NOSH Air Fryer

By Joy May & Tim May

cont

ents

Hello!

Thank you for picking up 'NOSH Air Fryer'. Whether you've been cooking with us for years or this is your very first NOSH book, you're so welcome!

Over the past year or so, we've seen just how many people are turning to air fryers for quick, easy, and more energy-efficient cooking. They're brilliant little machines, but we noticed that a lot of books focus on snacks and sides. We wanted to do something different.

This book is also a little special for another reason. It's the first NOSH book with Tim's name on the cover. Tim (my son, if you didn't already know) has been working with me on these books for over 20 years. He started by photographing recipes in the early days and gradually moved into recipe development, testing, and writing the odd recipe here and there. Now, he's moved beyond those early days and become an author in his own right.

We've always worked together as a family, and that's still such a special thing for us. Long may that continue. You'll be hearing a lot more from him in the years to come, and we can't wait to see what he comes up with next.

Right, enough about us, back to the book. We're so excited to share it with you and we really hope you love it as much as we do.

Happy cooking!

Joy & Tim

Our Mission...

To make cooking so simple people actually do it.

Welcome to Our Air Fryer Cookbook

Every cookbook we've written has had one simple goal: to help people cook with confidence, no matter where they are in their journey. Whether it's learning to cook for the first time, adapting to a new dietary need, or feeding a family, we aim to meet you where you are and make cooking easier.

So, when air fryers shot to fame, we knew this was a new way people were approaching cooking - and we wanted to help. But we also wanted to bring our own twist to the air fryer world.

What Makes This Book Different?

Our focus is on creating full meals using only an air fryer (okay, we do use a kettle now and then, but that doesn't really count, does it?). We also found that it can be tricky to get enough vegetables into air fryer meals, so we've made a conscious effort to include them wherever we can.

Our Approach

> Use only an air fryer for cooking.

> Create full meals for two people.

> Make sauces in the air fryer whenever possible.

> Include a photo with every recipe.

> Keep ingredients lists short and simple.

We hope this book helps you get the most out of your air fryer, without overcomplicating things. Let's get cooking!

a mug =

No need for weighing scales if you don't want to use them. Just grab a mug and get cooking. Cooking isn't about perfection; it's about getting tasty food on the table.

Throughout the book we have used a mug to measure ingredients. The mug holds ½ a pint (300ml) of liquid and is the size of the mug pictured opposite.

ACTUAL SIZE

intro
duc

Let's Talk Baskets

We like to keep things simple in this book. There are plenty of accessories available for air fryers - racks, skewers, silicone moulds, liners, and probably a whole load of things we haven't even come across. They might be great, but we prefer to stick to the basics.

For us, there are just two options:

1 **Crisper tray in** – This is the default. Leaving the crisper tray in allows hot air to circulate around your food, giving you those perfectly crispy results we all love.

2 **Crisper tray out** – When we make sauces, we'll tell you to remove the crisper tray, if needed.

Not all air fryer baskets are the same

In some air fryers, there aren't any baskets at all, only shelves. Others might have holes in the base or back, which makes cooking with any liquid tricky.

The solution is the same for all types: get yourself a loaf tin or a small tray that fits inside your basket or air fryer. This will help contain or catch any liquid used in our recipes.

Still unsure about baskets?

Scan for video

Let's Talk Temps & Times...

This is probably the elephant in the room when it comes to air fryers. Two people can cook the same thing, using the same settings, yet one ends up raw, while the other is burnt. How is that possible?

The big influencers

The truth is, several factors have a huge impact on how food cooks in an air fryer:

1 **Your Air Fryer Model** – Not all air fryers are created equal. Some run hotter and cook faster than others.

2 **Basket Size** – A larger basket will be less crowded and will allow more hot air to circulate around the food, so things may cook faster.

3 **Food Size & Thickness** – The bigger, or thicker, the food, the longer it takes to cook. This can lead to inconsistencies—one chicken breast might be done, while another needs extra time.

Of course, this variation isn't unique to air fryers. Traditional ovens vary in temperature, different baking trays conduct heat differently, and food itself naturally comes in different sizes. However, because air fryers cook much faster than conventional ovens, even small differences in time or temperature can have a significant impact.

So How Do We Handle This?

At first, you can't just set it and forget it. Instead, check on your food as it cooks. If your air fryer has a 'shake' reminder, use it as a prompt to take a peek. A visual check is one of the best ways to tell if something is done.

If you're unsure, try these simple tests:

1 Actually try your food before you serve it up. Test the **thickest** ingredient.

2 Cut into the **thickest** part of your meat to see if it's no longer pink.

3 Use a food thermometer to check the internal temperature of the middle of the thickest part of the meat or fish, avoiding bones. See p216 for temperatures.

4 If you find that food is browning too quickly before cooking through, reduce the temperature by 10°C next time.

Cooking times are a guide, not a rule.

We tested these recipes on a mid-range air fryer, so the times are fairly conservative. Your food may need a few more minutes, or it might cook slightly faster—just keep an eye on it, and you'll soon get a feel for how your air fryer behaves.

How to use a temperature probe
Scan for video

Our
Air Fryer

** We are _NOT_ sponsored by Cosori! **

Why Two Baskets?

Our goal with this book is to create complete meals using only an air fryer. While plenty of recipes work with a single basket, having two baskets makes it much easier to cook a full meal, including your protein, carbs, and veggies, all at the same time.

What If You Only Have One Basket?

No worries! You can still use this book, you might just need to cook some elements separately or use a saucepan here and there. We've included tips for single-basket air fryers in each recipe, where needed, so you'll never be left guessing. We've got you covered!

Only got one basket?
Scan for video

Shake & Check

Most foods need a shake...

For the best results, assume that most foods in the air fryer need a shake every few minutes, except for obvious exceptions like whole fish or eggs. If it makes sense for what you're cooking, give it a shake!

Check your food...

If your air fryer has a 'shake' reminder, use it. Shaking helps things crisp up evenly, and it also gives you a chance to check your food's progress. Our recipes include cooking times, but we often say things like 'until nicely browned' or 'until tender' — and the only way to know that is by checking.

Oil & Air Frying: Keep it Simple

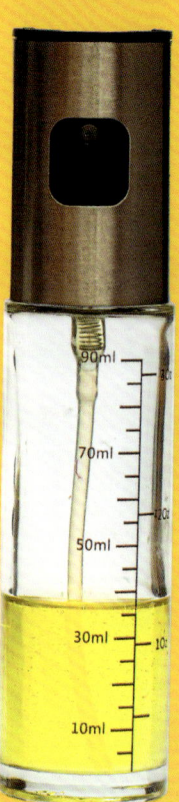

Which Oil Should You Use?

When it comes to oil, we're not here to tell you exactly what you should use. Olive oil, rapeseed oil, or any light cooking oil works well. However, avoid pre-made oil sprays. They often contain additives that you don't need, and some people say they can even damage your air fryer.

Spray or Toss?

There are two ways to use oil in an air fryer:

1 **Spraying** – A light spray helps food crisp up and prevents sticking.

2 **Tossing** – Tossing ingredients in a bowl, with a little oil before cooking, can give an even coating, especially for things like roast potatoes.

When to Spray?

We won't remind you every time you might need to spray, but here's a simple rule of thumb:

YES - If you want it crispy or brown, spray it.

NO - If it's wet or has plenty of liquid (like a stew), skip the oil.

Our take on using oil in your air fryer
Scan for video

A Brief Note on Settings

Not all air fryers are created equal. There are big ones, small ones, single or double baskets, tower models, front-loading, top-loading, you name it!

So which settings do you need to use?

One common question we hear is regarding the 'settings' people are using. The reality is that not every air fryer offers the same settings, and even when they do, the results can vary by brand. We could tell you to use your 'roast' or 'bake' setting, but you might not have those options, or they might work differently from ours.

...so we keep it simple

We **ONLY** use the 'air fry' setting and adjust the temperature as needed. It may not be perfect, but it should help everyone achieve similar results.

Air fryer settings we use

Scan for video

AIR FRY   ROAST   REHEAT

BAKE   GRILL   DRY

PRE HEAT   SHAKE

Accessories

Do You Really Need Extra Accessories?

You've just bought an air fryer, and now people are telling you to buy more stuff...well, yes and no. There aren't many 'must-haves', and chances are, you already own some of them!

The Essentials

> **Cooking tray** - A non-stick, low-sided tray that fits inside your basket.

> **Loaf tin** - We use a 3lb tin, as it fits perfectly. To check the size of yours, simply fill it with water and weigh it - 1,500g is roughly a 3lb tin.

> **Spray bottle** – A good one makes all the difference. Look for one with good reviews - some don't 'mist' oil well.

> **Fine grater** - A Microplane is ideal, but the small holes on a standard box grater work too.

Nice to Have

> **Thermometer** - Nothing fancy needed, but it's great for peace of mind when cooking meat.

> **Lifters** - Oven gloves work, but lifters can make things easier.

What You Don't Need

> **Silicone trays & moulds** - Air fryers are easy to clean, often easier than silicone itself.

> **Racks** - They take up more space than they save and don't make a huge difference.

Stick with the basics, and you'll be good to go!

Gadget tour

Scan for video and links

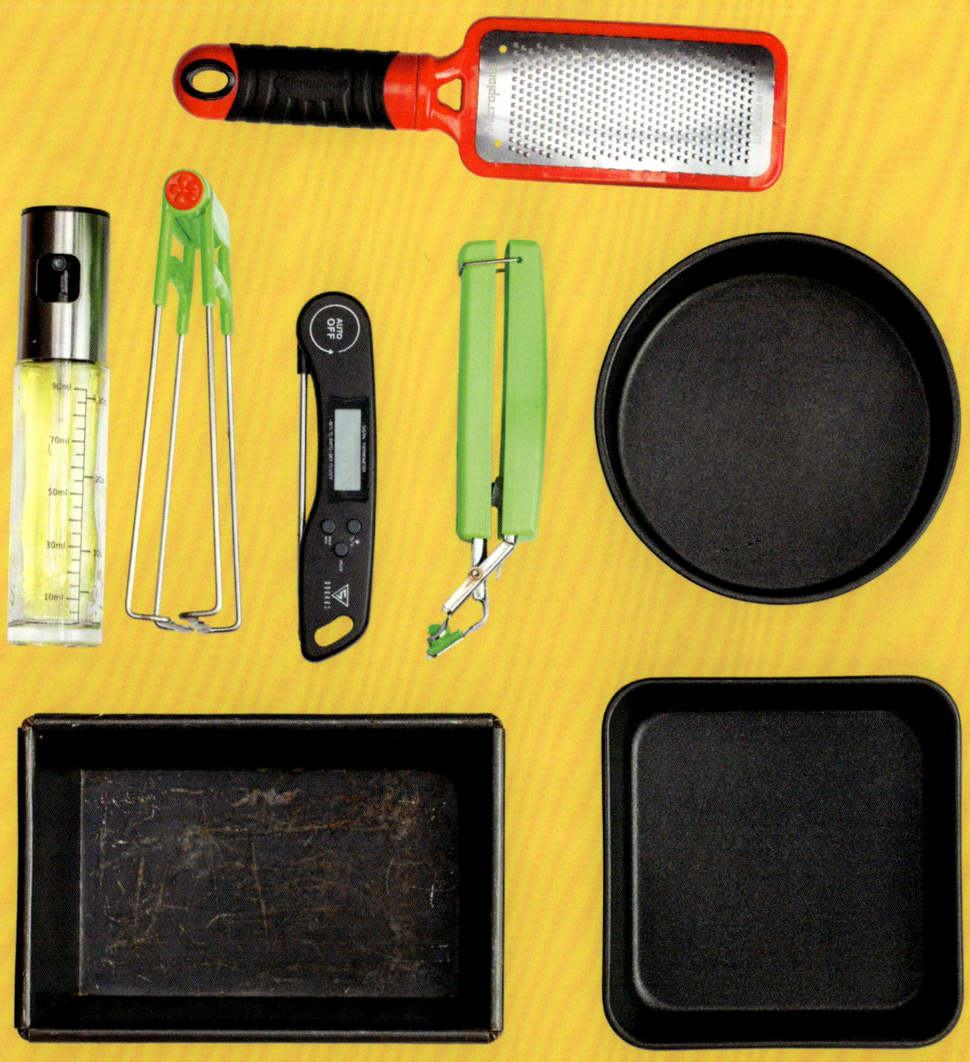

Cod Ratatouille

Ratatouille

1 **onion**, cut into wedges

1 **courgette**, cut into chunks

1 **red pepper**, cut into small chunks

125g **mushrooms**, halved

2 cloves **garlic**, finely grated

1 tablespoon **dried basil**

12 **black olives**, halved

3 **tomatoes**, chopped

1 tablespoon **olive oil**

2 tablespoons **cider vinegar**

2 **cod steaks**

8 **anchovy fillets**

1 In a mixing bowl, combine the ratatouille ingredients. Season well with salt and pepper.

2 Divide the mixture between the two baskets of your air fryer and air fry at 200°C for 15 minutes, or until the vegetables begin to brown.

3 Place the cod steaks on top of the cooked vegetables. Spray with a little oil, season with pepper, and air fry for 8 minutes, or until the cod is cooked through and begins to flake a little.

🌡 *Internal temperature 63°C*

4 Serve with the anchovies on top of the cod.

Single basket?

If you only have a single basket air fryer, add all the ratatouille ingredients to your basket and air fry for 5-10 minutes longer. Once done, remove and keep warm. Then air fry the cod on its own, using the same timing as in step 3.

Time	Serves	£/person
30 mins	2	£4.11

Salmon & New Potatoes

400g **new potatoes**, thinly sliced

5 **spring onions**, sliced

2 cloves **garlic**, finely grated

1 mug (150g) defrosted **frozen peas**

2 **salmon fillets**

Sour Cream Sauce

3 tablespoons **soured cream**

1 tablespoon freshly chopped **chives**

2 teaspoons **Dijon mustard**

1 Add the sliced potatoes to the air fryer basket and air fry at 200°C for 15 minutes, or until browned and cooked through.

2 Add the spring onions and garlic to the potatoes and air fry for another 5 minutes.

3 Stir in the peas.

4 Place the salmon fillets, skin side up, on top of the potato and pea mixture. Spray the salmon with oil, season with salt and pepper, and air fry for 8 minutes, or until cooked through and flakes easily.

🌡 *Internal temperature 50–63°C*

5 In a small bowl, mix together the sauce ingredients.

6 Serve the salmon and potatoes with the sour cream sauce.

Time	Serves	£/person
35 mins	2	£2.64

Mediterranean Sardines

2 **medium potatoes**, cut into small chunks

1 teaspoon **dried rosemary**

2 cloves **garlic**, finely grated

200g **cherry tomatoes**, halved

5 **spring onions**, chopped

400g tin **haricot beans**, rinsed and drained

200g **fresh skin-on sardines** or **fresh mackerel**

1 Add the potatoes, rosemary and garlic to the air fryer and air fry at 200°C for 10–15 minutes, or until the potatoes are cooked through and lightly browned.

2 Add the cherry tomatoes, spring onions and haricot beans and air fry for 5 minutes.

3 Arrange the sardines on top, skin side up, and air fry for an additional 5 minutes, or until the skin begins to crisp.

🌡 *Internal temperature 63°C*

Time	Serves	£/person
30 mins	2	£2.55

Fish & Chips

3 **medium potatoes**, cut into chips

2 slices **bread**

4 **anchovy fillets**

2 tablespoons **plain flour**

1 **egg**, beaten

2 **cod steaks**

1 mug (150g) defrosted **frozen peas**

3 tablespoons **mayo**

4 **sun-dried tomatoes**, chopped

1 In a large bowl, toss the potatoes in a little oil. Season with salt and pepper and air fry at 180°C for 20 minutes.

2 Meanwhile, add the bread, anchovies, some salt and pepper and a little oil to a food processor. Blitz until you have breadcrumbs.

3 Place the flour in one bowl, the beaten egg in a second bowl, and the anchovy-breadcrumb mix in a third bowl.

4 Dip each cod steak first in the flour, then the egg, then the anchovy-breadcrumb mix, pressing lightly to coat.

5 Add the fish to the air fryer on top of the chips and air fry at 200°C for 10 minutes, turning halfway through, or until nicely browned.
🌡 *Internal temperature 63°C*

6 Meanwhile, cook the peas, see p213.

7 Mix together the mayo and sun-dried tomatoes. Serve.

Time	Serves	£/person
30 mins	2	£2.82

Honey & Soy Salmon

¾ mug (190g) **basmati rice**

3 tablespoons **soy sauce**

3 tablespoons **honey**

2 **salmon fillets**

4 **spring onions**, chopped

1 **pak choi**, sliced

1 mug (150g) defrosted **frozen peas**

Single basket?

You'll need to cook your rice in a saucepan - see p210.

1 Cook the rice, see p210.

2 Meanwhile, in a bowl, mix the soy sauce and honey, then add the salmon and spring onions. Leave to marinate for 10 minutes.

3 When the rice has 8 minutes remaining, place the salmon and all the marinade in your second basket and air fry at 200°C for 6 minutes.
🌡 *Internal temperature 50–63°C*

4 Add the pak choi and air fry for a further 2 minutes.

5 Meanwhile, cook the peas, see p213, then stir them into the cooked rice.

6 Serve the rice and peas with the salmon on top. Pour any remaining marinade from the basket over the salmon.

Time	Serves	£/person
25 mins	2	£2.72

Rice in your air fryer

Scan for video

Salmon Gratin

2 **salmon fillets**, cut into bite-sized pieces

5 **spring onions**, chopped

1 mug (150g) defrosted **frozen peas**

½ mug (150ml) **double cream**

2 **medium potatoes**, very thinly sliced

1 mug (75g) grated **Gruyère cheese**

1 Remove the crisper tray from your air fryer.

2 Combine the salmon, spring onions, peas and double cream in the basket. Season with salt and pepper.

3 Toss the potato slices in a little oil. Arrange them on top of the salmon mixture. Season with salt and pepper. Air fry at 180°C for 20 minutes, or until the potatoes are brown and tender (test the thickest slice).

4 Sprinkle the grated Gruyère over the top and air fry for 3 minutes, or until the cheese has melted.

Time	Serves	£/person
30 mins	2	£3.30

Mackerel with Pancetta & Fennel

250g **new potatoes**, sliced

1 **courgette**, sliced

1 **red pepper**, sliced

1 **red onion**, cut into wedges

1 **small head of fennel**, 'fronds' (spikey bits) removed and cut into wedges

77g **pancetta lardons**

2 slices **bread**, made into breadcrumbs

1 teaspoon **olive oil**

½ mug (30g) grated **Parmesan**

2 **fresh mackerel fillets**

1 Toss the potatoes, courgettes, pepper, onion and fennel in a little oil. Spread across both air fryer baskets and air fry at 200°C for 15 minutes, or until the potatoes are tender.

2 Add the pancetta and air fry for a further 5 minutes.

3 Mix together the breadcrumbs, oil and Parmesan and press onto the top of the fish (skin side down).

4 Place the fish on top of the vegetables and pancetta, and air fry for 5 minutes, or until the topping is golden brown.

🌡 *Internal temperature 63°C*

Single basket?

A single basket might be a little crowded for the first step, so just allow an extra 10 minutes for that step.

Time	Serves	£/person
35 mins	2	£3.46

Salmon with Prik Nam Som

2/3 mug (160g) **basmati rice**

400ml tin **coconut milk**

3 tablespoons **white wine vinegar**

1 **fat green chilli**, finely sliced

1 tablespoon **Thai red curry paste**

2 **salmon fillets**

4 **spring onions**, chopped

100g **mangetout**, sliced lengthways

Single basket?

You'll need to cook your rice in a saucepan - see p210.

1 In a loaf tin, mix the rice and coconut milk. Cover tightly with foil and air fry at 200°C for 25 minutes. For more tips on cooking rice, see p210.

2 In a small bowl, combine the white wine vinegar and green chilli to make your Prik Nam Som. Set aside.

3 Spread the Thai red chilli paste over the salmon fillets. Set aside.

4 When the rice has 10 minutes remaining, add the salmon and spring onions to the second basket. Air fry at 200°C for 9 minutes, or until the salmon is slightly browned and cooked through.
🌡 *Internal temperature 50-63°C*

5 Meanwhile, cook the mangetout, see p213.

6 Serve the salmon on the coconut rice with the mangetout alongside. Drizzle the Prik Nam Som over everything just before serving.

Time	Serves	£/person
30 mins	2	£3.06

**Rice in your
air fryer**

Scan for video

Smoked Haddock & Prawn Bake

2 pieces **smoked haddock**, cut into bite-sized pieces

150g defrosted **frozen prawns**

5 **spring onions**, chopped

½ mug (150ml) **double cream**

3 **medium potatoes**, grated

1 teaspoon **olive oil**

1 Remove the crisper tray from your basket. Add the haddock, prawns, spring onions and double cream. Season with salt and pepper. Air fry at 200°C for 10 minutes.

2 Meanwhile, in a bowl, toss the grated potato with olive oil and season with salt and pepper.

3 Spread the potato evenly over the fish mixture. Air fry at 180°C for 10 minutes, or until the potato is nicely browned and crisp.

Time	Serves	£/person
25 mins	2	£3.44

Salmon Bites

4 **medium potatoes**, cut into wedges

2 tablespoons **curry paste**

2 **salmon fillets**, de-skinned and cut into chunks

1 tablespoon **mayo**

1 tablespoon **wholegrain mustard**

zest of ½ a **lemon**

1 slice **bread**

1 teaspoon **olive oil**

1 teaspoon **turmeric**

4 tablespoons **Greek yoghurt**

juice of ½ a **lemon**

1 Toss the potato wedges in the curry paste. Air fry at 180°C for 30 minutes or until nicely browned and tender.

2 In a bowl, mix the salmon with the mayo, mustard and lemon zest. Season with salt and pepper.

3 Put the bread, oil and turmeric in a food processor and blitz until you have breadcrumbs.

4 When the wedges have 10 minutes to go, put the salmon in the other basket and air fry at 200°C for 8 minutes or until lightly browned.
🌡 *Internal temperature 50-63°C*

5 Once cooked, very gently break up the salmon bites over the wedges.

6 Mix together the yoghurt and lemon and drizzle over the top.

Single basket?

Either add the salmon bites on top of the wedges at step 4, or air fry the wedges first, then remove and keep warm while you air fry the salmon bites.

Time	Serves	£/person
35 mins	2	£2.42

Thai King Prawn Soup

250g **king prawns** (fully defrosted if using frozen)

1 ½ mugs (450ml) **boiling water**

2 teaspoons **red Thai curry paste**

2 teaspoons **tamarind paste**

1 teaspoon **turmeric**

2 teaspoons **fish sauce**

juice of a **lime**

2 teaspoons **granulated sugar**

1 In a bowl, combine all the ingredients. Pour everything into the basket. Air fry at 200°C for 5 minutes, or until the prawns are lightly browned.

🌡 *Internal temperature 63°C*

2 Serve the prawns in a bowl and pour the liquid over the top.

Time	Serves	£/person
10 mins	2	£1.65

Katsu Chicken

³/₄ mug (190g) **basmati rice**

Katsu Sauce

1 **onion**, roughly chopped

1 **carrot**, roughly chopped

1 clove **garlic**, finely grated

1 teaspoon **curry powder**

1 teaspoon **turmeric**

1 **chicken stock cube**

400ml tin **coconut milk**

2 **chicken breasts**

1 ½ mugs (75g) **cornflakes**, crushed

Single basket?

You'll need to cook your rice in a saucepan - see p210.

---

1 Cook your rice, see p210.

2 With the crisper tray removed, air fry the onion, carrot and garlic at 200°C for 10 minutes, or until the onions begin to brown.

3 Flatten the chicken breasts using a heavy object (e.g. a rolling pin) until they are around 1cm thick.

4 Place the crushed cornflakes on a plate and season with salt and pepper. Press the chicken into the cornflakes to coat evenly.

5 Place the coated chicken on top of the vegetables in the air fryer and air fry at 200°C for 10 minutes or until nicely browed. Flip halfway through.
🌡 *Internal temperature 74°C*

6 Once the chicken is cooked, remove it from the basket and set to one side. Add the remaining sauce ingredients to the vegetables in the basket and air fry for 5 minutes until warmed through.

7 Blitz the sauce with a handheld blender until smooth.

8 Slice the chicken and serve with the rice and Katsu sauce.

Time	Serves	£/person
35 mins	2	£2.34

Rice in your air fryer

Scan for video

Sweet & Sour Chicken

Sauce

4 tablespoons **tomato ketchup**

4 tablespoons **mirin**

2 tablespoons **soy sauce**

1 tablespoon **brown sugar**

1 tablespoon **cornflour** mixed with 3 tablespoons **cold water**

1 **red pepper**, sliced

5 **spring onions**, roughly chopped

1 clove **garlic**, finely grated

2 **chicken breasts**, sliced

300g **straight-to-wok noodles**

1 In a large bowl, mix together the sauce ingredients until smooth.

2 Mix in the rest of the ingredients, apart from the noodles.

3 Pour into the basket and air fry at 200°C for 10 minutes, or until the chicken begins to brown a little.

🌡 *Internal temperature 74°C*

4 In another bowl, cover the noodles in boiling water, leave for 5 minutes, then drain.

5 Serve the cooked chicken on top of the drained noodles and pour over the remaining sauce from the basket.

Time	Serves	£/person
25 mins	2	£2.79

Honey Mustard Chicken

400g **new potatoes**, cut into chunks

2 **medium carrots**, peeled and chopped

4 **skin-on chicken thighs**

Topping

5 **spring onions**, sliced

2 cloves **garlic**, finely grated

½ mug (150ml) **single cream**

1 **chicken stock cube**, crumbled

1 teaspoon **dried basil**

1 tablespoon **wholegrain mustard**

1 tablespoon **honey**

1 mug (150g) defrosted **frozen peas**

1 In a bowl, toss the potatoes and carrots in a little oil and air fry at 180°C for 25 minutes or until the potatoes are golden and and the carrots are cooked through.

2 After 10 minutes of the potatoes cooking, in the second basket, add the chicken thighs, skin side down, and air fry at 200°C for 15 minutes, then turn over.

🌡 *Internal temperature 74°C*

3 Meanwhile, in a bowl, mix together the topping ingredients. Pour over the chicken and air fry for 10 minutes, or until the chicken is browned on top.

4 Cook your peas, see p213.

Single basket?

At point 2, add the chicken on top of the veg, but allow 20 minutes for the chicken to air fry. Remove the chicken and leave the veg in for another 10 minutes if needed.

Time	Serves	£/person
30 mins	2	£1.81

Sriracha Honey Burger

3 **medium potatoes**, cut into chips

2 tablespoons **plain flour**

1 **egg**, beaten

1 tablespoon **sriracha sauce**

1 tablespoon **honey**

2 slices **bread**, made into breadcrumbs

4 small **skinless, boneless chicken thighs**, laid out flat

2 tablespoons **sriracha sauce**

3 tablespoons **mayo**

1 **Little Gem lettuce**, thinly sliced

¼ **small red onion**, very thinly sliced

5 **cherry tomatoes**, sliced

2 **brioche burger buns**

1 In a bowl, toss the chips in a little oil and season with salt and pepper. Air fry at 180°C for 20 minutes or until nicely browned.

2 Arrange three bowls: one with the flour, another with a mixture of the egg, sriracha and honey, and a final bowl with the breadcrumbs.

3 Starting with the flour, then the egg mixture, and finally the breadcrumbs, dip the chicken in each and finish by pressing in the breadcrumbs to fully coat.

4 Air fry at 190°C for 15 minutes or until nicely browned and cooked through.
🌡 *Internal temperature 74°C*

5 Mix together the sriracha and mayo to make a sauce. Serve everything together.

Single basket?

Air fry the chips first, then remove and cover with foil to keep warm while the chicken cooks. If needed, reheat the chips in the air fryer for a few minutes, after the chicken is cooked.

Time	Serves	£/person
35 mins	2	£2.97

Creamy Chicken

400g **new potatoes**, halved

2 **chicken breasts**

150g **mushrooms**, halved

150g **green beans**, trimmed

1 **white wine stock pot**

300ml **double cream**

1 tablespoon freshly chopped **basil**

Single basket?

Let the potatoes air fry for 15 minutes before adding the chicken. After step 2 the potatoes should be fully cooked, remove everything - including the crisper tray - and keep warm while you finish the remaining steps.

1 Toss the potatoes in a little oil, season with salt and pepper and air fry at 180°C for 10 minutes.

2 Add the chicken on top and air fry for a further 10 minutes, or until the chicken is cooked through.

3 Meanwhile, in the other basket with the crisper tray removed, air fry the mushrooms at 200°C for 5 minutes.

4 Add the beans, stock pot and cream to the mushrooms and air fry for 10 minutes, or until the beans are tender.

5 Once cooked, remove the chicken. Continue cooking the potatoes if they need more browning.

🌡 *Internal temperature 74°C*

6 Slice the chicken and mix into the sauce along with the basil.

Time	Serves	£/person
25 mins	2	£2.79

Texas BBQ Chicken with Loaded Fries

4 **medium potatoes**, cut into chips

400g tin **black beans**, rinsed and drained

2 **chicken breasts**

6 rashers **bacon**

BBQ sauce

3 tablespoons **ketchup**

1 tablespoon **honey**

1 tablespoon **Worcestershire sauce**

1 teaspoon **smoked paprika**

1 mug (75g) grated **Cheddar cheese**

1 **fat green chilli**, sliced (or jarred jalapeños)

2 tablespoons **mayo**

1 teaspoon **honey**

1 teaspoon **hot sauce** (optional)

1 Toss the potatoes in a little oil, season with salt and pepper and air fry at 180°C for 20 minutes or until browned. Add the black beans and air fry for another 3 minutes.

2 Meanwhile, wrap the chicken breasts in the bacon rashers.

3 In a small bowl, combine the BBQ sauce ingredients.

4 Spread a third of the sauce over the chicken breasts and air fry in your other basket at 200°C for 10 minutes. Check every few minutes to add a little more sauce each time.
🌡 *Internal temperature 74°C*

5 Add the grated cheese and sliced chillis over the chips, air fry for 3 minutes.

6 Mix together the mayo, honey and hot sauce (add small amounts at a time depending on how hot you like it) and drizzle over the top of everything to serve.

Single basket?

Let the chips air fry for 15 minutes before increasing the temperature to 200°C and adding the chicken on top. Once the chicken is cooked, remove it, add the beans, and air fry for 3 minutes before adding the grated cheese to melt.

Time	Serves	£/person
40 mins	2	£2.82

Toby's Chicken Fajitas

1 **small red onion**, sliced

2 cloves **garlic**, finely grated

1 **red pepper**, thinly sliced

2 **chicken breasts**, sliced

3 tablespoons **soy sauce**

2 teaspoons **smoked paprika**

2 teaspoons **mild chilli powder**

2 teaspoons **ground cumin**

2 tablespoons **tomato purée**

1 **Little Gem lettuce**, thinly sliced

4 **tortilla wraps**

+ whatever else you like in fajitas!

1 Toss the onion, garlic and red pepper in a little oil and air fry at 200°C for 5 minutes, or until the onion begins to brown.

2 In a bowl, mix together the chicken, soy sauce, paprika, chilli, cumin and tomato purée.

3 Add the chicken on top of the vegetables, spread it out, and air fry for 10 minutes, or until the chicken is nicely browned.
🌡 *Internal temperature 74°C*

4 Fill the wraps with the cooked chicken, lettuce and whatever else you like in fajitas.

Who's Toby?

Ben's eldest son really wanted to write a recipe for this book, so he played around with his favourite fajita recipe - and we ended up with this little beauty! Well done Toby!

Time	Serves	£/person
20 mins	2	£2.55

Chicken & 'White Wine' Pie

1 **onion**, chopped

2 **medium carrots**, chopped into small chunks

4 **skinless, boneless chicken thighs**, cut into bite-sized chunks

1 tablespoon **plain flour**

1 **white wine stock pot**

1 mug (300ml) **boiling water**

2 **medium potatoes**, very thinly sliced

200g **mangetout**, sliced

1 With the crisper tray removed, air fry the onions and carrots at 180°C for 12 minutes, or until the onions begin to soften.

2 Add the chicken and air fry for 8 minutes, or until the chicken begins to brown.

3 Stir in the flour.

4 Add the stock pot, boiling water, and season with salt and pepper.

5 In a single layer, arrange the potatoes on top, spray with oil, and season well with salt and pepper. Air fry for 20 minutes, or until the potatoes are browned and cooked through (check by testing the thickest potato).

6 Cook the mangetout, see p213.

Time	Serves	£/person
45 mins	2	£3.21

Thai Coconut Chicken

1 **red onion**, cut into wedges

1 **medium sweet potato**, cut into small chunks

400ml tin **coconut milk**

3 tablespoons **red Thai curry paste**

4 **skin-on chicken thighs**

³/₄ mug (190g) **basmati rice**

1 **chicken stock cube**

100g **sprouting broccoli**

¹/₃ mug (60g) **cashews**

Single basket?

You'll need to cook your rice and broccoli separately in saucepans - see p210 & p213.

1 Toss the onion and sweet potato in a little oil and air fry at 200°C for 15 minutes, or until the sweet potato is cooked through.

2 In a bowl, mix together the coconut milk, curry paste and chicken thighs.

3 Add the chicken thighs, skin side down, on top of the sweet potato. Pour over the rest of the coconut milk mixture and air fry for 10 minutes. Turn over the chicken and air fry for a further 10 minutes or until nicely browned and cooked through.

4 Meanwhile, in the other basket, cook the rice with the stock cube crumbled in, see p210. After 20 minutes, add the broccoli into the rice container, cover and air fry for a final 8 minutes.

5 Once the chicken is nicely browned, add the cashews and air fry for 3 more minutes to brown the nuts a little.

🌡 *Internal temperature 74°C*

6 Pour the sauce from the basket over the top when serving.

	Time	Serves	£/person
68	45 mins	2	£2.83

**Rice in your
air fryer**

Scan for video

Garlic Lemon Chicken

2 slices **seeded bread**

1 clove **garlic**, finely grated

1 sprig **rosemary**, stalk removed and leaves chopped

1 teaspoon **olive oil**

2 **chicken breasts**

Salad

1 bag **salad**

150g **cherry tomatoes**, halved

1 **avocado**, sliced

5cm piece **cucumber**, sliced

10 **black olives**, halved

½ **lemon**, cut into wedges

1 Put the bread, garlic, rosemary and oil in a food processor and blitz to make breadcrumbs.

2 Bash the chicken breasts between two sheets of baking paper until ½cm thick.

3 Cover the chicken in the breadcrumbs and press in firmly.

4 Air fry at 200°C for 6 minutes or until golden brown.
Internal temperature 74°C

5 Serve with the combined salad ingredients with a squeeze of lemon over the top.

	Time	Serves	£/person
70	20 mins	2	£2.72

Chicken Pad Thai

Sauce

2 tablespoons **tamarind paste**

2 tablespoons **honey**

1 tablespoon **fish sauce**

2 tablespoons **oyster sauce**

2 **chicken breasts**, sliced

1 **small onion**, chopped

1 clove **garlic**, finely grated

¼ mug (40g) **peanuts**

2 **eggs**, beaten

100g **beansprouts**

300g **thick straight-to-wok noodles**

1 **lime**, cut into wedges

Single basket?

You can either use a frying pan to gently fry the beaten egg for step 2, or cook the eggs first in the air fryer, as per step 2, and set to one side, covered, while everything else cooks.

---

1 In a large bowl, mix together the sauce ingredients and add the chicken, onion, garlic and peanuts. Air fry at 200°C for 10 minutes, or until the chicken is cooked through and begins to brown.

2 Meanwhile, add the eggs into a shallow non-stick baking tin with a spray of oil. Cover with foil and air fry in your second basket at 200°C for 10 minutes, or until the egg is set. Remove from the tray and slice.

3 Once the chicken is cooked, add the beansprouts and air fry for 3 minutes to warm through.
🌡 *Internal temperature 74°C*

4 In a large bowl, pour boiling water over the noodles to warm through for 3 minutes. Drain when tender.

5 Combine everything together and serve with a squeeze of lime over the top. Pour any excess sauce from the basket (you might need to remove the crisper tray to get it all, sorry!).

Time	Serves	£/person
30 mins	2	£2.94

Miso Chicken Noodles

Miso chicken

1 teaspoon **toasted sesame oil**

2 **chicken breasts**, sliced

1 **red pepper**, sliced

1 tablespoon freshly grated **ginger**

2 tablespoons **miso paste**

2 tablespoons **soy sauce**

1 tablespoon **honey**

100g **mangetout**, thinly sliced

300g **straight-to-wok noodles**

1 In a large bowl, mix together the miso chicken ingredients.

2 Air fry at 200°C for 10 minutes, or until the chicken is browned and cooked through.
🌡 *Internal temperature 74°C*

3 In another bowl, cover the mangetout and noodles in boiling water for 3–4 minutes. Drain.

4 Serve with the chicken. Pour over any sauce from the bottom of the crisper tray. Add a few tablespoons of boiling water into the basket to thin down the sauce if it has boiled away.

Time	Serves	£/person
15 mins	2	£2.96

Honey & Thyme Chicken with Veg Frites

Veg Frites

1 **medium sweet potato**, cut into chips

1 **medium parsnip**, cut into chips

1 **medium carrot**, cut into chips

3 tablespoons **ground almonds**

2 **large chicken legs** (drumstick and thigh together)

2 tablespoons **honey**

1 tablespoon freshly chopped **thyme**

zest and juice of ½ a **lemon**

1. In a bowl, toss the veg frite ingredients with a little oil and air fry at 180°C for 20 minutes or until nicely browned and tender (check the carrots in particular).

2. Meanwhile, toss the rest of the ingredients together and air fry, skin side down, in your second basket at 190°C for 10 minutes.

3. Turn the chicken over and continue to air fry for a further 15 minutes or until nicely browned and cooked through.
   🌡 *Internal temperature 74°C*

4. Serve with any sauce left in the bottom of the basket poured over.

Single basket?

Air fry your frites first, then remove and set aside while the chicken cooks. Once the chicken is done, remove it and reheat the frites in the air fryer for a few minutes while the chicken rests.

Time	Serves	£/person
40 mins	2	£3.96

Chorizo Stuffed Chicken & Mash

4 **medium potatoes**

²/₃ mug (40g) freshly grated **Parmesan**

25g **butter**

2 **chicken breasts**

100g **chorizo**, sliced

1 tablespoon **Cajun seasoning**

150g **tenderstem broccoli**

Single basket?

You'll need to cook your mash and broccoli separately in saucepans - see p215 & p213.

1 Make your mash, see p215. Once mashed, stir in the Parmesan and butter.

2 Meanwhile, make small slits or pockets in the chicken and stuff with sliced chorizo.

3 Sprinkle the Cajun seasoning over the chicken and air fry at 200°C for 10 minutes or until nicely browned and cooked through.
🌡 *Internal temperature 74°C*

4 Once your potatoes are out of the air fryer (if you're using that method), cook your broccoli, see p213.

Time	Serves	£/person
50 mins	2	£3.46

Mash in your air fryer

Scan for video

Harissa Chicken & Potato Rosti

4 **mushrooms**

1 **small onion**

2 tablespoons **harissa paste**

2 **chicken breasts**

100g **asparagus**

3 **medium potatoes**, grated

3 tablespoons **mayo**

2 **small gherkins**, chopped

Single basket?

Air fry the rosti first, then remove and cover with foil to keep warm while the chicken cooks. Reheat in the air fryer for a few minutes after the chicken is cooked, if needed.

1 In a food processor, blitz the mushrooms, onion and harissa paste into a paste.

2 Make shallow cuts in the chicken breasts and cover with the paste. Season well and spray with oil. Set to one side.

3 Form the grated potatoes into two piles. Spray with oil, season with salt and pepper, and air fry at 180°C for 7 minutes. Turn over and air fry for a further 7 minutes, or until nicely browned all over.

4 Meanwhile, air fry the chicken in your second basket at 200°C for 6 minutes, along with the asparagus. Turn over and air fry for a further 6 minutes or until nicely browned and cooked through. Check your asparagus and remove if cooked.

🌡 *Internal temperature 74°C*

5 Mix together the mayo and gherkins and serve over the top.

Time	Serves	£/person
20 mins	2	£2.58

Tandoori Chicken & Bombay Potatoes

Bombay potatoes

3 **medium potatoes**, cut into chunks

1 teaspoon **mustard seeds**

1 teaspoon **mild chilli powder**

1 teaspoon **turmeric**

Tandoori chicken

1 tablespoon freshly grated **ginger**

2 cloves **garlic**, finely grated

1 teaspoon **ground cumin**

1 teaspoon **ground coriander**

1 teaspoon **garam masala**

1 teaspoon **ground cinnamon**

100ml **Greek yoghurt**

4 **skinless, boneless chicken thighs**

100ml **Greek yoghurt**

2 tablespoons **mango chutney**

1 In a large bowl, mix the Bombay potato ingredients with a little oil. Season well and air fry at 180°C for 20 minutes, or until the potatoes are browned and cooked through.

2 Meanwhile, in another bowl, mix the Tandoori chicken ingredients together. Air fry in your second basket, at 200°C for 18 minutes, turning halfway, or until nicely browned and cooked through.

🌡 *Internal temperature 74°C*

3 Mix the yoghurt and mango chutney together and serve everything together.

Single basket?

Air fry the potatoes first, then remove and cover with foil to keep warm while the chicken cooks. If needed, reheat the potatoes in the air fryer for a few minutes, after the chicken is cooked.

Time	Serves	£/person
25 mins	2	£2.62

Garlic Chilli Chicken

4 **skinless, boneless chicken thighs**, cut into chunks

Sauce

1 tablespoon **cornflour**

1 tablespoon **honey**

1 tablespoon **Gochujang paste**

1 tablespoon **mirin**

2 tablespoons **soy sauce**

1 **fat red chilli**, chopped (deseeded if you don't want it too spicy)

4 cloves **garlic**, finely grated

5 tablespoons **water**

4 **spring onions**, chopped

1 **pak choi**, chopped

300g **straight-to-wok noodles**

1 Mix the chicken with the sauce ingredients.

2 Transfer to an air fryer and air fry at 200°C for 8 minutes, or until the chicken begins to brown.
🌡 *Internal temperature 74°C*

3 On top, add the spring onions and pak choi and air fry for 3 minutes.

4 Meanwhile, pour boiling water over your noodles, leave for 3 minutes, and drain.

5 Serve everything together. Pour the sauce from the basket over the top.

Time	Serves	£/person
20 mins	2	£3.18

Smoked Paprika Chicken Nuggets

4 **medium potatoes**, cut into chips

6 **cherry tomatoes**

2 slices **bread**, made into breadcrumbs

1 teaspoon **smoked paprika**

2 **chicken breasts**, cut into pieces

1 **egg**, beaten

1 teaspoon **tomato purée**

1 teaspoon **honey**

Single basket?

Air fry the chips first, then remove and cover with foil to keep warm while the chicken cooks. If needed, reheat the chips in the air fryer for a few minutes, after the chicken is cooked.

1 Toss the chips in a little oil, season with salt and pepper, and air fry at 180°C for 20 minutes or until browned and cooked through.

2 Put the tomatoes in a small ramekin or tray and air fry, in your second basket, at 200°C for 5 minutes or until they start to brown. Once cooked, remove from the air fryer and set to one side.

3 Meanwhile, mix the breadcrumbs and paprika together. Spray the breadcrumbs with oil and mix together. Season well with salt and pepper.

4 Dip the chicken in the beaten egg, then press into the breadcrumbs to coat.

5 In your second basket, air fry at 200°C for 5 minutes, turn over, and air fry for another 5 minutes depending on how thick you have cut the chicken pieces.
🌡 *Internal temperature 74°C*

6 While the chicken is cooking, add the tomato purée and honey to the tomatoes and blitz until smooth.

Time	Serves	£/person
30 mins	2	£1.89

Chicken Char Sui

Marinade

2 tablespoons **soy sauce**

2 cloves **garlic**, finely grated

2 tablespoons **honey**

2 tablespoons **hoisin sauce**

1 teaspoon **Chinese five-spice**

4 **skinless, boneless chicken thighs**

¾ mug (190g) **basmati rice**

1 **pak choi**, chopped

1 teaspoon **toasted sesame oil**

1 teaspoon **sesame seeds** (optional)

Single basket?

You'll need to cook your rice in a saucepan - see p210.

---

1 Combine the marinade ingredients and add the chicken thighs. Leave for as long as you have time (anything up to 24 hours, but 10 minutes is fine).

2 Cook the rice, see p210.

3 Meanwhile, place the chicken, smooth side down, in the basket and air fry at 200°C for 8 minutes.

4 Flip over and pour over any excess marinade. Air fry for another 8 minutes or until nicely browned and cooked through. Remove and set to one side to rest.
🌡 *Internal temperature 74°C*

5 Toss the pak choi in the sesame oil and air fry at 200°C for 3 minutes to soften slightly.

6 Serve with the sesame seeds sprinkled over the top (optional).

Time	Serves	£/person
30 mins	2	£2.70

Rice in your air fryer

Scan for video

Jerk Chicken

³/₄ mug (190g) **basmati rice**

¹/₂ teaspoon **ground allspice**

¹/₂ 400g tin **kidney beans**, rinsed and drained

Jerk chicken

2 **chicken breasts**, sliced

1 tablespoon **jerk seasoning**

juice of a **lime**

2 cloves **garlic**, finely grated

1 tablespoon freshly chopped **thyme**

1 **Scotch bonnet chilli**, finely chopped

2 **spring onions**, finely chopped

1 **lime**, cut into wedges

1 Cook the rice along with the allspice and beans, see p210. You might need an extra 5 minutes of cooking time. Just check and return to the air fryer if needed.

2 Meanwhile, in a large bowl, combine the jerk chicken ingredients.

3 When the rice has 5 minutes to go, air fry the chicken at 200°C for 8 minutes or until nicely browned.
Internal temperature 74°C

4 Serve everything together with lime juice over the rice.

Single basket?

You'll need to cook your rice in a saucepan - see p210.

Time	Serves	£/person
30 mins	2	£2.25

Rice in your air fryer

Scan for video

Classic Caeser Salad

1 **large chicken breast**

4 rashers **bacon**

1 teaspoon **olive oil**

1 clove **garlic**, finely grated

2 slices **thick cut white bread**, cut into chunks

Dressing

6 **anchovy fillets**, chopped

4 tablespoons **mayo**

juice of ½ a **lemon**

2 teaspoons **Dijon mustard**

½ mug (30g) finely grated **Parmesan**

1 **Romaine lettuce**, chopped

8 **anchovy fillets**

a few shavings (with a peeler) of **Parmesan**

1 Season the chicken with salt and pepper and spray with a little oil. Air fry at 200°C for 10 minutes or until lightly browned.
🌡 *Internal temperature 74°C*

2 After 2 minutes, add the bacon and air fry together for the remaining 8 minutes. Remove and set to one side.

3 Meanwhile, in a large bowl, mix the oil and grated garlic. Add the chunks of bread and mix to coat in the garlic oil.

4 Air fry the bread at 200°C for 3 minutes or until browned.

5 Roughly chop the chicken and bacon and mix with the combined dressing ingredients and lettuce.

6 Serve with anchovies and croutons on top and any extra Parmesan you like.

Time	Serves	£/person
25 mins	2	£3.46

Thai Chicken Fried Rice

³/₄ mug (190g) **basmati rice**

1 **red pepper**, sliced

2 cloves **garlic**, finely grated

2 **chicken breasts**, cut into bite-sized pieces

1 tablespoon freshly grated **ginger**

1 teaspoon **toasted sesame oil**

2 tablespoons **fish sauce**

2 tablespoons **soy sauce**

2 tablespoons **maple syrup**

5 **spring onions**, finely chopped

200g tin **sweetcorn**, drained

1 **pak choi**, sliced

1 **fat red chilli**, finely chopped (optional)

1 Cook the rice, see p210.

2 In a large bowl, toss the pepper, garlic, chicken and ginger in the sesame oil.

3 With the crisper tray removed, air fry at 200°C for 8 minutes or until the chicken begins to brown.

🌡 *Internal temperature 74°C*

4 Add the cooked rice and the rest of the ingredients, mix together and air fry for 4 minutes to warm through.

Single basket?

You'll need to cook your rice in a saucepan – see p210.

Time	Serves	£/person
35 mins	2	£3.07

Rice in your
air fryer
Scan for video

veg
aria

Paneer & Squash Tikka

1 **small butternut squash**, cut into small chunks

1 **small red onion**, cut into wedges

¾ mug (190g) **basmati rice**

100g **paneer cheese**, cut into chunks

2 cloves **garlic**, finely grated

2 tablespoons **tikka curry paste**

400ml tin **coconut milk**

4 tablespoons **ground almonds**

1 tablespoon freshly chopped **coriander**

1 Toss the butternut and onion in a little oil and air fry at 200°C for 15 minutes, or until the butternut is tender.

2 Meanwhile, cook the rice, see p210.

3 Mix together the paneer, garlic, curry paste, coconut milk and ground almonds. Add to the butternut and air fry for 10 minutes, or until the paneer is browned a little.

4 Serve with the rice and garnish with coriander. Pour over the sauce from the bottom of the basket.

Single basket?

You'll need to cook your rice in a saucepan – see p210.

Time	Serves	£/person
30 mins	2	£2.10

Rice in your air fryer

Scan for video

Harissa Sweet Potato

1 **red onion**, chopped

2 cloves **garlic**, finely grated

1 **medium sweet potato**, cut into small chunks

½ mug (150ml) **boiling water**

1 **vegetable stock cube**

400g tin **chickpeas**, rinsed and drained

400g tin **puy lentils**, rinsed and drained

2 tablespoons **harissa paste**

100g **fresh spinach**, chopped

1 Toss the onion, garlic and sweet potato in a little oil, with the crisper tray removed. Air fry at 200°C for 15 minutes, or until the sweet potatoes are browned and cooked through.

2 Add the rest of the ingredients, apart from the spinach, and return to the air fryer for 5 minutes or until heated through. Season with salt and pepper.

3 Stir in the chopped spinach. It should wilt.

Time	Serves	£/person
25 mins	2	£2.92

Quinoa & Kale Burger

1 **small onion**, cut into wedges

2 cloves **garlic**, finely grated

100g **kale**

2 slices **bread**

250g **ready-cooked quinoa**

6 **sun-dried tomatoes**

1 **egg**

2 **brioche burger buns**

1/2 **small red onion**, very thinly sliced

2 tablespoons **mayo**

1/4 bag **salad**

1 Air fry the onion and garlic at 200°C for 5 minutes.

2 Meanwhile, add the kale to a large bowl and cover with boiling water. Leave for 2 minutes, then drain.

3 Add the kale on top of the onions and air fry for 3 minutes to dry out the kale a little.

4 Put the bread in a food processor and blitz until you have rough breadcrumbs.

5 Add the onion, garlic and kale to the food processor along with the quinoa, sun-dried tomatoes and egg. Season well with salt and pepper. Blitz together to combine.

6 Form into 2 burgers. Spray with oil and air fry at 200°C for 8 minutes, or until the burger is nicely browned.

7 Serve with the red onion, mayo and salad leaves.

Time	Serves	£/person
30 mins	2	£1.98

Greek Frittata

6 **spring onions**, chopped

10 **black olives**, halved

6 **eggs**

1 tablespoon freshly chopped **basil**

200g **cherry tomatoes**, halved

100g **feta**, chopped

Single basket?

Either do one portion at a time, one after another. Alternatively, at point 3, add all the ingredients to a larger dish and allow a little more time to cook the egg.

1 Add an ovenproof dish or shallow cooking tin to each basket.

2 Add the spring onions and olives to each dish and air fry at 200°C for 2 minutes.

3 In a mixing bowl, beat together the eggs and basil. Share between each dish and air fry for 2 minutes.

4 Stir gently from the sides, then air fry for another 2 minutes. Repeat until the egg is no longer runny.

5 Once the egg is almost completely set, add the tomatoes and feta over the top and air fry for 2 minutes, or until the feta browns lightly.

Time	Serves	£/person
25 mins	2	£1.07

Rogan Josh

20g **butter**

1 **small red onion**, chopped

6 **mushrooms**, sliced

¾ mug (190g) **basmati rice**

400ml tin **coconut milk**

2 tablespoons **rogan josh curry paste**

50g **fresh spinach**, roughly chopped

2 **eggs**

Single basket?

Once you've cooked the rice curry, leave it, covered with foil, in the tin, while you cook the eggs. It should stay plenty warm.

1 Place a loaf tin in your air fryer. Add the butter, onion and mushrooms, and air fry at 200°C for 5 minutes, or until the mushrooms begin to brown.

2 Add the rice, coconut milk and curry paste, and stir together.

3 Tightly cover your pan with foil and air fry for 25 minutes. All the liquid should be absorbed and the rice tender.

4 Remove the foil and stir in the spinach. Season with salt and pepper.

5 Meanwhile, add the eggs in their shells to your second basket and air fry at 130°C for 10 minutes.

6 Once the eggs are cooked, immediately transfer to a bowl of cold water to cool, then gently crack the shells all over and peel.

Time	Serves	£/person
35 mins	2	£1.01

Leek, Potato & Camembert

25g **butter**

1 **leek**, sliced

150g **mushrooms**, sliced

100ml **crème fraîche**

1 tablespoon **Dijon mustard**

3 **medium potatoes**, very thinly sliced

150g **sprouting broccoli**

150g **Camembert**, sliced

Single basket?

You'll need to cook your broccoli in a saucepan – see p213.

1 With the crisper tray removed, add the butter and leeks and air fry at 180°C for 7 minutes until the leeks begin to brown

2 Add the mushrooms and air fry for 2 minutes.

3 Mix in the crème fraîche and mustard and season well with salt and pepper.

4 Layer the potatoes on top, season with salt and pepper, and spray with oil. Air fry for 20 minutes.

5 With 10 minutes remaining, cook your broccoli, see p213.

6 Once the potatoes are browned and cooked through, layer the Camembert on top and return to the air fryer for 2 minutes, or until the cheese begins to brown.

Time	Serves	£/person
40 mins	2	£2.07

Broccoli in your air fryer

Scan for video

Greens Risotto

25g **butter**

1 **medium leek**, sliced

³/₄ mug (190g) **basmati rice**

1 ½ mugs (450ml)
boiling water

1 **veg stock cube**, crumbled

100g **sprouting broccoli**,
roughly chopped

100g **garlic and herb
cream cheese**

50g **kale**, roughly chopped

150g **Cambazola** or **Brie**, sliced

1 Place a loaf tin in your air fryer. Add the butter and leeks and air fry at 200°C for 5 minutes, or until the leeks begin to brown.

2 Add the rice, water and stock cube. Cover tightly with foil and air fry for 18 minutes, or until most of the liquid has been absorbed into the rice.

3 Carefully remove the foil and add the broccoli. Replace the foil and air fry for another 6 minutes.

4 Stir in the Philadelphia cream cheese and kale. Cover again and air fry for 3 minutes.

5 Serve with the cheese on top.

Time	Serves	£/person
40 mins	2	£2.55

Beetroot & Halloumi Couscous

1 **red onion**, cut into wedges

2 **raw beetroots**, peeled and cut into wedges

1 **red pepper**, cut into chunks

1 mug (300ml) **boiling water**

1 **veg stock cube**

½ mug (100g) **couscous**

150g **cherry tomatoes**

10 **black olives**, halved

200g **halloumi**, sliced

1 tablespoon freshly chopped **basil**

1 Toss the onion, beetroot and peppers in a little oil and air fry at 180°C for 15 minutes, or until the beetroot is tender.

2 Meanwhile, in a bowl, combine the boiling water and stock cube. Add the couscous and cover with a plate for 5-10 minutes. All the water should get absorbed.

3 Once the beetroot is tender, add the tomatoes, olives and halloumi and air fry for a further 5 minutes, or until the halloumi is nicely browned.

4 Serve the couscous with the roasted veg on top. Garnish with the chopped basil.

Time	Serves	£/person
25 mins	2	£2.27

Green Chilli Burgers with Mango Chutney

1 **fat green chilli**

1 tablespoon freshly grated **ginger**

1 **medium carrot**, peeled and cut into chunks

1 tablespoon freshly chopped **coriander**

1 slice **bread**

1 **medium potato**, grated

½ mug (75g) defrosted **frozen peas**

2 **brioche burger buns**

coleslaw

mango chutney

1 Put the chilli, ginger, carrot, coriander and bread in a food processor and blitz. Season well with salt and pepper.

2 Add the potato and peas and pulse a couple of times to combine.

3 Form into two burgers.

4 Air fry at 200°C for 12 minutes, turning halfway, or until nicely browned.

5 Serve with the buns, coleslaw and mango chutney.

Time	Serves	£/person
25 mins	2	£0.74

Gochujang Aubergines

³/₄ mug (190g) **basmati rice**

1 **large aubergine**, sliced

1 **red pepper**, sliced

100g **baby corn**, halved

1 clove **garlic**, finely grated

1 tablespoon freshly grated **ginger**

1 tablespoon **soy sauce**

1 tablespoon **gochujang paste**

1 tablespoon freshly chopped **coriander**

1 Cook the rice, see p210.

2 Toss together the aubergine, pepper, corn, garlic, ginger, soy sauce and gochujang with a little oil.

3 Air fry at 200°C for 15 minutes or until nicely browned.

4 Serve with the rice and coriander.

Single basket?

You'll need to cook your rice in a saucepan – see p210.

Time	Serves	£/person
30 mins	2	£1.67

Rice in your air fryer
Scan for video

Sweet Potato & Lentil Curry

³/₄ mug (190g) **basmati rice**

2 **medium sweet potatoes**, cut into small chunks

1 **onion**, sliced

1 teaspoon **ground cumin**

1 teaspoon **ground coriander**

½ teaspoon **ground turmeric**

400ml tin **coconut milk**

400g tin **cooked green lentils**, rinsed and drained

juice of a **lime**

1 tablespoon freshly chopped **coriander**

Single basket?

You'll need to cook your rice in a saucepan – see p210.

1 Cook the rice, see p210.

2 Toss the sweet potato, onion, cumin, coriander and turmeric in a little oil.

3 With the crisper tray removed, air fry at 200°C, stirring occasionally, for 20 minutes, or until the sweet potato is tender (test a few bits).

4 Add the coconut milk and lentils. Air fry for 5 minutes or until warmed through. Stir in half of the lime juice.

5 Serve with the rice, coriander and the rest of the lime juice to taste.

Time	Serves	£/person
35 mins	2	£1.44

Rice in your air fryer

Scan for video

Chilli & Basil Cob Platter

2 **medium courgettes**, quartered lengthways

2 **red peppers**, quartered

2 **corn on the cobs**, halved

juice of a **lime**

1 teaspoon **dried chilli flakes**

Dressing

2 tablespoons freshly chopped **basil**

1 clove **garlic**, finely grated

juice of ½ a **lemon**

1 Air fry the courgettes and peppers at 200°C for 15 minutes or until nicely browned.

2 Meanwhile, in the other basket, spray the corn with a little oil and air fry at 200°C for 10 minutes. Once cooked, squeeze over the lime juice and sprinkle with chilli flakes.

3 Mix together (or blitz) the dressing ingredients.

Single basket?

Air fry the corn first and wrap in foil to keep warm while you cook the rest of the vegetables.

Time	Serves	£/person
25 mins	2	£2.03

Miso Butternut & Mirin Mushrooms

Miso squash

1 **medium butternut squash**, chopped into chunks

1 tablespoon freshly grated **ginger**

1 clove **garlic**, finely grated

1/4 teaspoon **dried chilli flakes**

1 tablespoon **miso paste**

Honey mushrooms

4 **large Portobello mushrooms**

1 tablespoon **honey**

1 tablespoon **mirin**

1 tablespoon **soy sauce**

50g **fresh spinach**, roughly chopped

250g **ready-cooked puy lentils**

juice of 1/2 a **lime**

1 In a large bowl, combine the miso squash ingredients. Air fry at 200°C for 20 minutes or until nicely browned.

2 When the squash has 10 minutes remaining, combine the honey mushroom ingredients. In a separate basket, air fry at 200°C for 10 minutes.

3 In a large bowl, mix the squash together with the spinach and puy lentils.

4 Squeeze the juice of the lime over everything, and serve.

Single basket?

Air fry the miso squash and combine with the spinach, lentils and lime. Cover the bowl with foil to keep warm while the mushrooms cook.

Time	Serves	£/person
30 mins	2	£3.14

Simple Tomato Soup

1 **red onion**, cut into wedges

250g **cherry tomatoes**

1 clove **garlic**, left whole and unpeeled

1 **veg stock cube**

1 mug (300ml) **boiling water**

1 tablespoon freshly chopped **basil**

2 tablespoons **crème fraîche**

crusty bread

1 Toss the onion, tomatoes and whole garlic in a little oil. Season with salt and pepper, then air fry at 200°C for 10 minutes, or until the onions are browned a little.

2 Tip the contents of the air fryer into a large bowl. Squeeze the garlic from its skin, add the rest of the ingredients and blitz with a handheld blender.

3 Serve with crusty bread.

	Time	Serves	£/person
124	15 mins	2	£0.81

Baked Gnocchi

250g **gnocchi**

5 **spring onions**, chopped

250g **cherry tomatoes**, halved

400g tin **butter beans**, rinsed and drained

15g **sun-dried tomatoes**, roughly chopped

100g **fresh spinach**, roughly chopped

75g ball **mozzarella**, torn into pieces

1 Toss the gnocchi in a little oil and air fry at 200°C for 8 minutes, or until lightly browned. Season well with salt and pepper.

2 Stir in the remaining ingredients, except the mozzarella.

3 Layer the mozzarella on top and air fry for 5 minutes, or until the mozzarella is melted and browned.

Time	Serves	£/person
20 mins	2	£1.65

Tear & Share Steak Salad

2 **thick beef steaks**

1 tablespoon **Dijon mustard**

½ teaspoon freshly ground **black pepper**

1 tablespoon **honey**

ciabatta loaf, sliced

1 clove **garlic**

Salad

1 **Little Gem lettuce**, leaves left whole

200g **cherry tomatoes**, halved

100g **blue cheese**, roughly chopped

Dressing

1 tablespoon **extra virgin olive oil**

1 tablespoon **balsamic vinegar**

1 teaspoon **honey**

1 tablespoon freshly chopped **basil**

1 Cover the steaks in the mustard, pepper and honey. Set to one side.

2 Air fry the ciabatta at 200°C for 5 minutes or until lightly browned.

3 Remove and rub with the clove of garlic.

4 Air fry the steaks at 200°C for 7 minutes or until they reach your preferred internal temperature, see chart below.

5 Remove the steaks, leave to rest for a couple of minutes, then slice.

6 Serve with the salad and combined dressing ingredients.

Steaks - Internal Temperatures

Steaks will continue to cook a little, even after you take them out of the air fryer, so it's best to remove the steak 2°C before it reaches the temperatures here – it should rise to those figures while resting.

Rare – 50°C
Medium Rare – 55°C
Medium – 60°C
Medium Well – 65°C
Well done – 70°C

Time	Serves	£/person
25 mins	2	£6.15

Using a temp probe
Scan for video

Smash Burger

4 **medium potatoes**, cut into chips

250g **minced beef**

½ **small red onion**, thinly sliced

Cheddar cheese, thinly sliced

2 **brioche buns**, sliced and toasted

1 **Cos lettuce**, thinly sliced

+ whatever sauces or relishes you desire

Single basket?

Air fry the chips first, then remove and cover with foil to keep warm while the burger cooks. Reheat the chips in the air fryer for a few minutes after the burger is cooked.

---

1 Toss the chips in a little oil, season well, and air fry at 180°C for 20 minutes or until nicely browned.

2 Season the mince with salt and pepper and mix together with your hands.

3 Split the meat into two balls and place each on a small square (20cm x 20cm) of baking paper. Place the sliced onions on top and press down with your hands until nice and thin.

4 While the meat and onions are still on the baking paper, air fry at 200°C for 4 minutes, or until the onions begin to brown.

5 Using a fish slice, carefully flip over and remove the baking paper. Air fry for another 2 minutes.
🌡 *Internal temperature 70°C*

6 Turn the burgers again and add the cheese. Return to the air fryer for 1 minute, just to melt the cheese.

7 Serve with the lettuce and the sauces of your dreams.

Time	Serves	£/person
25 mins	2	£1.68

Beef, Bacon & Bean Bake

1 **small onion**, chopped

250g **minced beef**

1 **beef stock cube**

½ mug (150ml) **boiling water**

1 tablespoon **tomato purée**

150g **cherry tomatoes**

400g tin **cannellini beans**, rinsed and drained

3 **medium potatoes**, grated

150g **sprouting broccoli**

1 mug (75g) grated **Gruyère cheese**

100g **streaky bacon**

Single basket?

You'll need to cook your broccoli in a saucepan –
see p213.

1 With the crisper tray removed, air fry the onion at 200°C for 3 minutes or until it begins to soften.

2 Add the mince and air fry for 8 minutes, or until the mince begins to brown. Stir every couple of minutes and break up the mince.

3 Add the stock cube, boiling water, tomato purée, cherry tomatoes and cannellini beans. Air fry for 5 minutes to warm through.

4 Spread the grated potato over the meat mixture, season well with salt and pepper, spray with oil and air fry at 180°C for 10 minutes, or until the potato is slightly browned.

5 Meanwhile, cook your broccoli, see p213.

6 Sprinkle the grated cheese over the top, then add the bacon. Air fry for 8 minutes, or until the bacon is lightly browned.

Time	Serves	£/person
40 mins	2	£3.46

Broccoli in your air fryer
Scan for video

Crispy Fried Shredded Beef

250g **beef steak** (sirloin), thinly sliced

1 **egg**, beaten

4 tablespoons **cornflour**

Sauce

2 cloves **garlic**, finely grated

1 tablespoon freshly grated **ginger**

1 **red pepper**, sliced

4 tablespoons **sweet chilli sauce**

2 tablespoons **soy sauce**

2 tablespoons **rice wine vinegar**

4 tablespoons **tomato ketchup**

300g **straight-to-wok noodles**

1 **spring onion**, finely chopped

1 tablespoon **sesame seeds** (optional)

1 In a bowl, mix the beef with the beaten egg.

2 In a separate bowl, add the cornflour, season well with salt and pepper, and mix. Add the beef to the cornflour mixture to coat.

3 Air fry the beef at 200°C for 8 minutes, or until browned.

4 Meanwhile, to make the sauce, remove the crisper tray from the second basket. Add the garlic, ginger and red pepper to the basket and air fry at 200°C for 5 minutes.

5 Stir in the rest of the sauce ingredients and air fry for another 5 minutes to heat through.

6 Place the noodles in a mixing bowl, cover with boiling water and leave to soak for 5 minutes. Drain.

7 Add the cooked beef to the sauce and stir to combine.

8 Serve with the noodles, chopped oions, and the optional sesame seeds.

Single basket?

Make the sauce first (steps 4 and 5) and set to one side. Replace the crisper tray and cook the beef (steps 1, 2 and 3).

Time	Serves	£/person
25 mins	2	£3.89

Swedish Meatballs

3 **medium potatoes**, cut into wedges

1 teaspoon **smoked paprika**

Meatballs

250g **minced beef**

1 **small onion**

1 clove **garlic**, finely grated

1 slice **bread**

½ teaspoon **ground allspice**

1 tablespoon freshly chopped **parsley**

Sauce

1 tablespoon **Worcestershire sauce**

1 teaspoon **wholegrain mustard**

½ mug (150ml) **soured cream**

1 mug (150g) defrosted **frozen peas**

1 Toss the wedges in a little oil with the paprika and season with salt and pepper. Air fry at 180°C for 20 minutes or until nicely browned.

2 Meanwhile, put the meatball ingredients in a food processor and blitz until smooth.

3 With oil on your hands, form the mixture into 12 meatballs.

4 Air fry the meatballs in your second basket at 200°C for 8 minutes, or until they begin to brown.
🌡 *Internal temperature 70°C*

5 Mix together the sauce ingredients, pour over the meatballs and air fry for a further 3 minutes to warm through.

6 Cook your peas, see p213.

> ## Single basket?
>
> Air fry the wedges first, then remove and cover with foil to keep warm while the meatballs cook. If needed, reheat the wedges in the air fryer.

	Time	Serves	£/person
138	30 mins	2	£1.47

Chipotle Buritos

250g **minced beef**

1 **small red onion**, chopped

1 **red pepper**, chopped

1 teaspoon **ground cumin**

2 tablespoons **chipotle paste**

400g tin **black beans**, rinsed and drained

2 **tomatoes**, roughly chopped

1 tablespoon **red wine vinegar**

4 **tortilla wraps**

1 mug (75g) grated **Cheddar cheese**

1 With the crisper tray removed, air fry the mince, onion and pepper at 200°C for 10 minutes or until nicely browned.

2 Add the cumin, chipotle paste, black beans, tomatoes and vinegar and air fry for another 10 minutes until warmed through.

3 Distribute the mixture between the wraps, sprinkle the cheese over the top and wrap up.

4 Optional step: with the crisper trays added back in, spray the filled wraps with oil and air fry for 2–3 minutes or until lightly browned.

Time	Serves	£/person
30 mins	2	£2.44

Beef Chimichurri

Chimichurri Sauce

2 tablespoons freshly chopped **parsley**

2 tablespoons freshly chopped **coriander**

1 **small onion**, finely chopped

1 clove **garlic**, finely grated

2 tablespoons **red wine vinegar**

3 tablespoons **olive oil**

1 teaspoon **dried chilli flakes**

1 tablespoon **chipotle paste**

2 **beef steaks**, thinly sliced

3 **medium potatoes**, cut into chips

1 In a bowl, mix together the Chimichurri sauce ingredients.

2 In a separate bowl, combine half the Chimichurri sauce with the steak. Set to one side until needed.

3 Toss the chips in a little oil, season with salt and pepper and air fry at 180°C for 20 minutes or until nicely browned.

4 When the chips are browned, add the beef and sauce to your second basket and air fry at 200°C for 8 minutes or until browned.
🌡 *Internal temperature 55–70°C*

5 In a large bowl, toss everything together along with the rest of the sauce.

Single basket?

Air fry the chips first, then remove and cover with foil to keep warm while the steak cooks. If needed, at the end, reheat the chips in the air fryer.

Time	Serves	£/person
35 mins	2	£5.25

Beef Casserole

3 **medium potatoes**, halved

3 **carrots**, cut into chunks

1 **red onion**, sliced

2 cloves **garlic**, finely grated

250g **minced beef**

1 tablespoon **plain flour**

1 tablespoon **Worcestershire sauce**

2 teaspoons **Dijon mustard**

1 **red wine stock pot**

1 mug (300ml) **boiling water**

1 mug (150g) defrosted **frozen peas**

Single basket?

Air fry the potatoes and carrots first until completely cooked. Remove the potatoes and carrots, along with the crisper tray, and set aside. Fry the onions and remaining ingredients. Once the meat mixture is cooked, place the potatoes and carrots on top to warm through for 5 minutes before serving.

1 'Hassleback' your potatoes by placing a chopstick on both sides of each halved potato. Slice down to the chopsticks, creating multiple slits but without cutting all the way through.

2 Air fry the potatoes and carrots at 180°C for 35 minutes or until browned and cooked through. If your carrots cook faster than your potatoes, you can take them out while you wait for the potatoes to finish.

3 Meanwhile, remove the crisper tray from your second basket and air fry the onion and garlic at 200°C for 5 minutes, or until the onion begins to soften.

4 Add the minced beef and air fry for 10 minutes or until browned. Season well with salt and pepper.

5 Sprinkle the flour over the mixture and stir to combine. Air fry for 2 minutes.

6 Stir in the Worcestershire sauce, mustard, red wine stock pot and boiling water. Air fry for 10 minutes to heat through. Stir in your cooked carrots.

7 Cook your peas, see p213.

Time	Serves	£/person
40 mins	2	£1.55

How to
'hassleback'
Scan for video

Mongolian Beef

¾ mug (190g) **basmati rice**

200g **beef steak**, thinly sliced

Sauce

1 tablespoon freshly grated **ginger**

1 clove **garlic**, finely grated

5 **spring onions**, chopped

2 tablespoons **soy sauce**

1 tablespoon **cornflour**

2 tablespoons **brown sugar**

1 teaspoon **dried chilli flakes**

¼ mug (75ml) **boiling water**

1 Cook your rice, see p210.

2 In a bowl, add the beef to the combined sauce ingredients.

3 Add the boiling water and mix.

4 Air fry the beef and sauce at 200°C for 10 minutes or until browned.
🌡 *Internal temperature 55–70°C*

5 When serving, pour over the sauce from the bottom of the basket.

Single basket?

You'll need to cook your rice in a saucepan - see p210.

Time	Serves	£/person
30 mins	2	£2.66

Rice in your air fryer

Scan for video

Italian Pork Belly

4 medium **potatoes**

25g **butter**

1/2 mug (30g) grated **Parmesan**

1 clove **garlic**, left whole
and unpeeled

2 **carrots**, roughly chopped

1 stick **celery**, chopped

1 **onion**, cut into wedges

250g **pork belly**

1 **white wine stock pot**

1/2 mug (150ml) **boiling water**

Single basket?

You'll need to make your
mash using a saucepan -
see p215.

1 Make the mash, see p215. At the end, stir in
the butter and Parmesan.

2 Air fry the garlic, carrots, celery and onion at
200°C for 15 minutes or until they begin
to brown.

3 Pat the pork belly dry with kitchen towel and
season well. Add the pork belly on top of the
vegetables and air fry for a further 15 minutes,
or until the skin is nice and crispy. Remove the
pork and leave to rest.
🌡 *Internal temperature 77°C*

4 In a mixing bowl, disolve the stock pot in the
boiling water.

5 Squeeze the garlic from its skin and discard
the skin. Add to the stock, along with the rest
of the cooked vegetables and blitz
until smooth.

6 Serve with your pork belly and
mashed potatoes.

Time	Serves	£/person
50 mins	2	£1.57

Mash in your air fryer

Scan for video

Pork & Prunes with Boulangère Potatoes

3 **medium potatoes**, thinly sliced

1 **onion**, thinly sliced

1 tablespoon freshly chopped **parsley**

1 **white wine stock pot** + 1 mug (300ml) **boiling water**

25g **butter**, cut into cubes

1 **bay leaf**

1 sprig **thyme**

300ml **double cream**

2 **pork steaks**

8 **prunes**

Single basket?

Make the Boulangère potatoes and re-cover with foil once cooked. Set aside while you cook the pork and prunes.

1 In a large bowl, mix together the potatoes, onion and parsley along with half of the combined stock pot and boiling water.

2 Transfer to a shallow baking tin, place the butter on top and cover with foil. Air fry at 180°C for 25 minutes. Check if the potatoes are tender; if not, return for another 5 minutes.

3 Remove the foil and air fry for a further 15 minutes, or until the potatoes are nicely browned.

4 Remove the crisper tray from your second basket. Pour in the remaining stock, bay leaf, thyme and double cream.

5 Loosely replace the crisper tray and add the pork steaks and prunes. Spray with oil, season well and air fry at 200°C for 10 minutes or until cooked through.
🌡 *Internal temperature 75°C*

6 Serve the potatoes and steak with the sauce poured over.

Time	Serves	£/person
55 mins	2	£2.26

Bangers & Baked Potato Mash

4 **medium potatoes**

25g **butter**

6 **sausages**

1 **red onion**, cut into wedges

1 tablespoon **plain flour**

1 mug (300ml) **boiling water**

1 **beef stock cube**

1 teaspoon **honey**

1 teaspoon **Worcestershire sauce**

10 **cherry tomatoes**

Single basket?

You'll need to make your mash using a saucepan – see p215.

1 Make the mash, see p215. Stir in the butter and season well.

2 Meanwhile, in the other basket, with the crisper tray removed, air fry the sausages and onions at 200°C for 15 minutes, or until the sausages are fully cooked.
🌡 *Sausage internal temperature 71°C*

3 Remove the sausages, cover and set aside.

4 Stir the flour into the onions and air fry for 2 minutes.

5 Add the boiling water, crumbled stock cube, honey and Worcestershire sauce, stirring well. Air fry for 5 minutes, stirring occasionally, until the gravy thickens.

6 Add the cherry tomatoes to the basket that had the potatoes in (if you air fried them) and air fry at 200°C for 5 minutes.

7 Serve the sausages with the mashed potato, roasted cherry tomatoes and onion gravy.

Time	Serves	£/person
50 mins	2	£1.36

Mash in your air fryer

Scan for video

Chorizo Salad

125g **chorizo**, sliced

crusty bread, cut into croutons

1/2 **small red onion**, thinly sliced

200g **cherry tomatoes**, halved

1 bag **salad**

Dressing

1 teaspoon **capers**,
roughly chopped

1 tablespoon **red wine vinegar**

1 tablespoon **extra virgin
olive oil**

1 teaspoon **honey**

1 Air fry the chorizo at 200°C for 5 minutes.

2 In a bowl, add the bread and onion. Pour over
the chorizo, including any oil from the basket,
and toss everything together.

3 Return to the basket and air fry at 200°C for
4 minutes, or until the bread is nice and crispy.

4 Serve with the tomatoes, salad leaves and the
combined dressing ingredients over the top.

Time	Serves	£/person
15 mins	2	£1.74

Mexican Bean & Sausage Stew

400g tin **chopped tomatoes**

2 teaspoons **smoked paprika**

1 teaspoon **ground cumin**

1 teaspoon **ground coriander**

1 tablespoon **honey**

400g **kidney** or **borlotti beans**, do not drain the water unless salted

6 **sausages**

1 **onion**, cut into wedges

1 **red pepper**, cut into chunks

crusty bread

Single basket?

At the beginning, air fry your sausages, onion and red pepper and set to one side, until you add the sausages back in at the end.

1 Remove the crisper tray from one basket. Add the tinned tomatoes, smoked paprika, ground cumin, ground coriander and honey.

2 If your beans come in unsalted water, add the beans with their water directly to the sauce. If your beans are in salted water, drain and rinse them, then add the beans along with a quarter of a tin's worth of fresh water. Air fry at 200°C for 20 minutes, or until the sauce is hot.

3 Meanwhile, in the second basket, air fry the sausages, onion and red pepper at 200°C for 20 minutes, or until everything is nicely browned.
🌡 *Sausage internal temperature 71°C*

4 Once cooked, remove the sausages and cut into chunks.

5 Add the sausage pieces and roasted vegetables to the basket with the sauce. Stir everything together and serve with crusty bread.

Time	Serves	£/person
30 mins	2	£1.66

Red Cabbage & Sausage Hash

3 **potatoes**, cut into small chunks

1 **onion**, sliced

6 **sausages**

½ **small red cabbage**, thinly sliced

½ mug (150ml) **boiling water**

1 **chicken stock cube**

2 tablespoons **cider vinegar**

1 tablespoon **honey**

400g tin **cannellini beans**, rinsed and drained

1 With the crisper tray removed, air fry the potatoes and onions at 200°C for 25 minutes, or until the potatoes are cooked through.

2 Squeeze the sausages out of their skins and pinch into about 4 balls per sausage. Add to the basket and air fry for 10 minutes or until browned. Season with salt and pepper.

🌡 *Sausage internal temperature 71°C*

3 Add the cabbage, boiling water, stock cider vinegar and honey. Season with salt and pepper. Air fry for 5 minutes, or until the cabbage begins to soften.

4 Add the beans and air fry for a further 5 minutes.

Time	Serves	£/person
50 mins	2	£1.69

Chorizo & Squash Crumble

1 **small butternut squash**, cut into small chunks

150g **chorizo**, sliced

1 **onion**, roughly chopped

1 clove **garlic**, finely grated

½ mug (150ml) **double cream**

Topping

2 slices **bread**, made into breadcrumbs

½ mug (40g) grated **Cheddar cheese**

1 tablespoon **sesame seeds**

2 tablespoons **pumpkin seeds**

1 teaspoon **olive oil**

Single basket?

Air fry the butternut and set to one side. Then continue onto step 2.

1 Air fry the butternut at 180°C for 20 minutes or until tender and lightly browned.

2 Meanwhile, in the second basket with the crisper tray removed, air fry the chorizo, onion and garlic at 200°C for 10 minutes, or until the onion softens.

3 Add the cooked butternut to the basket with the chorizo, pour in the cream and mix. Air fry for 5 minutes.

4 Mix together the topping ingredients with a little oil. Spread over the contents of the basket and air fry for 5 minutes, or until the topping is nicely browned.

Time	Serves	£/person
35 mins	2	£2.28

Apple & Hoisin Pork Steaks

3 tablespoons **honey**

5 tablespoons **hoisin sauce**

2 **pork steaks**

1 **apple**, sliced

2 **medium potatoes**, cut into small chunks

1 **medium sweet potato**, cut into small chunks

2 **pak choi**, chopped

Single basket?

Air fry the potatoes first, then remove and cover with foil to keep warm while the pork steak cooks. At the end, if needed, reheat the potatoes in the air fryer.

1 In a bowl, mix together the honey and hoisin. Add the pork steaks and apple and leave to marinate until needed.

2 Toss the potatoes and sweet potato in a little oil and air fry at 180°C for 20 minutes or until browned and tender.

3 In the second basket, air fry the pork steaks and apple slices (reserving any excess marinade in the bowl) at 200°C for 6 minutes.

4 After 6 minutes, turn the pork steaks over and baste with some of the reserved marinade. Air fry for another 6 minutes.

5 Turn the pork steaks over one final time, pour over the remaining marinade and air fry for a further 5 minutes or until fully cooked and caramelised.
🌡 *Pork internal temperature 75°C*

6 Toss the pak choi in a bowl with a little oil and season with salt and pepper. Add the pak choi to the basket once the potatoes are done and air fry for 2 minutes.

7 Serve everything together, making sure to pour over the sauce from the basket.

Time	Serves	£/person
40 mins	2	£1.99

Brie & Pancetta Tatiflette

300g **new potatoes**, thinly sliced

1 **red onion**, sliced

100g **pancetta lardons**

1 **white wine stock pot**

³/₄ mug (225ml) **boiling water**

200g **Brie**, sliced

crusty bread

1 Toss the potatoes in a little oil and air fry at 180°C for 20 minutes or until they begin to brown.

2 Add the onions and air fry for 5 minutes.

3 Add the pancetta, stock and boiling water and air fry for 5 minutes, or until the potatoes are completely tender.

4 Place the sliced Brie on top and air fry for 3 minutes, or until the Brie is nicely melted.

5 Serve with crusty bread and pour over the liquid from the bottom of the basket.

Time	Serves	£/person
40 mins	2	£3.70

English Breakfast Hash

1 **onion**, cut into wedges

6 **sausages**, skins removed and each pinched into 4 pieces

6 rashers **bacon**, roughly chopped

4 **eggs**, beaten

1 teaspoon **sumac**

200g **cherry tomatoes**

1 **fat red chilli**, sliced

Single basket?

Either you can simply cook your scrambled egg gently in a frying pan (set to one side and cover in foil), or air fry at the end when everything else is cooked.

1 Air fry the onion and sausages at 200°C for 10 minutes, or until everything begins to brown.

2 Add the bacon and air fry for 5 minutes, or until it begins to brown.

3 Meanwhile, in a shallow non-stick baking tin in your second basket, add a little oil, then add the egg and sumac and mix. Air fry at 200°C for 2 minutes and stir. Repeat until the egg is set.

4 Add the cherry tomatoes to the onion, sausage and bacon basket and air fry for another 5 minutes.
🌡 *Sausage internal temperature 71°C*

5 Serve the hash with the eggs on the side. Garnish with sliced chilli.

Time	Serves	£/person
35 mins	2	£1.82

Yaku Soba Noodles

2 **pork steaks**, thinly sliced

1 **small onion**, thinly sliced

Sauce

1 tablespoon freshly grated **ginger**

4 tablespoons **Worcestershire sauce**

2 tablespoons **soy sauce**

2 tablespoons **oyster sauce**

1 tablespoon **mirin**

1 **small Chinese cabbage**, thinly sliced

1 **carrot**, very finely sliced

50g **beansprouts**

300g **straight-to-wok noodles** (Yaku soba if you can find them)

pickled sushi ginger (optional)

1 In a large bowl, mix the pork and onions with the combined sauce ingredients. Air fry at 200°C for 10 minutes, or until the pork begins to brown.

2 Add the cabbage, carrot and beansprouts and air fry for 5 minutes, or until the cabbage begins to soften.

3 Meanwhile, in a large bowl, cover the noodles in boiling water. Leave for 3 minutes, then drain.

4 Return the drained noodles to the bowl along with the contents of the basket and combine.

5 Serve with a few slices of pickled ginger

Time	Serves	£/person
20 mins	2	£2.68

Pigs & Blankets

(not Pigs _in_ Blankets)

6 **sausages**

1 **red onion**, cut into wedges

100g **streaky bacon**

1/3 mug (100ml) **boiling water**

1 **chicken stock cube**

1 tablespoon **cider vinegar**

1 teaspoon **honey**

150g **cherry tomatoes**

400g tin **cannellini beans**, rinsed and drained

2 slices **bread**, buttered and cut into chunks

1 Air fry the sausages and onions at 200°C for 10 minutes, or until the sausages begin to brown.

2 Add the bacon and air fry for 5 minutes, or until the bacon begins to brown.

3 Mix together the boiling water, stock cube, cider vinegar and honey, then add to the basket.

4 Add the tomatoes, beans and bread on top and air fry for 5 minutes, or until the bread is browned.

🌡 _Sausage internal temperature 71°C_

5 Remember to pour over the sauce from the bottom of the basket when you serve.

	Time	Serves	£/person
172	25 mins	2	£1.81

Moroccan Lamb Chops

1 **veg stock cube**
1 mug (300ml) **boiling water**
1/2 mug (100g) **couscous**

Spice mix
1 tablespoon **smoked paprika**
1 tablespoon **ground cumin**
1 tablespoon **ground coriander**
1/2 teaspoon **ground allspice**
1 teaspoon **mild chilli powder**

4 **lamb chops**
1 **courgette**, chopped
1 **red pepper**, chopped
4 tablespoons **Greek yoghurt**
1 tablespoon freshly chopped **mint**
juice of 1/2 a **lemon**
10 **apricots**, chopped

Single basket?

Air fry the vegetables first and mix with the cooked couscous to warm through before serving.

1 In a large bowl, disolve the stock cube in the boiling water. Add the couscous, cover the bowl with a plate, and set to one side.

2 In another bowl, combine the spice mix ingredients. Season with salt and pepper and set 2 tablespoons aside in a separate bowl to later make your yoghurt dip.

3 Add the lamb chops to the remaining spice mix and coat well.

4 Air fry the lamb at 200°C for 6 minutes, turn over and air fry for another 4 minutes or until nicely browned.
🌡 *Internal temperature 60-70°C*

5 Meanwhile, in the other basket, air fry the courgette and pepper at 200°C for 8 minutes, or until the courgette begins to brown.

6 Combine the yoghurt, mint and lemon juice with the reserved spice mix.

7 Mix the veg and the apricots with the cooked couscous and serve everything together.

Time	Serves	£/person
25 mins	2	£3.88

Lamb & Paneer Madras

¾ mug (190g) **basmati rice**

1 **lamb stock cube**

½ teaspoon **turmeric**

1 **small red onion**, sliced

250g **minced lamb**

125g **mushrooms**, sliced

3 **tomatoes**, chopped

2 tablespoons **Madras curry paste**

2 tablespoons **Greek yoghurt**

100g **paneer cheese**, chopped

Single basket?

You'll need to cook your rice in a saucepan – see p210.

---

1 Cook the rice, see p210, but add the stock cube and turmeric to the boiling water before mixing it with the rice.

2 Meanwhile, in your other basket, with the crisper tray removed, air fry the onions and lamb at 200°C for 10 minutes, stirring occasionally, until the mince is browned.

3 Add the mushrooms, tomatoes and curry paste. Air fry for 5 minutes.

4 Stir in the yoghurt and cooked rice with the lamb mixture.

5 Place the paneer over the top and air fry for 5 minutes, or until the cheese begins to brown.

Time	Serves	£/person
30 mins	2	£2.78

Rice in your air fryer

Scan for video

Lamb & Feta Bake

1 **medium sweet potato**, cut into small chunks

1 **onion**, chopped

2 cloves **garlic**, chopped

250g **minced lamb**

½ mug (150ml) **boiling water**

1 **lamb stock cube**

½ teaspoon **ground cinnamon**

2 teaspoons **smoked paprika**

1 tablespoon **tomato purée**

Topping

⅓ mug (100ml) **double cream**

1 **egg**, beaten

100g **feta**, crumbled

1 Toss the sweet potato in a little oil and air fry at 180°C for 15 minutes or until browned and cooked through. Once cooked, set to one side.

2 Meanwhile, in the other basket, with the crisper tray removed, air fry the onion, garlic and mince at 200°C for 10 minutes, stirring occasionally, until the mince is browned. Season well with salt and pepper.

3 Mix in the boiling water, stock cube, cinnamon, paprika, tomato purée and the cooked sweet potatoes.

4 In a bowl, mix together the topping ingredients and pour over the top.

5 Reduce the temperature to 180°C and air fry for 10 minutes, or until the top is nicely browned.

Single basket?

Air fry the sweet potatoes first, then remove them and take out the crisper tray. Continue onto step 2, cooking everything in sequence rather than side by side.

Time	Serves	£/person
30 mins	2	£2.25

Lamb Kebabs

Kebab

1 **small onion**, quartered

250g **lamb mince**

1 teaspoon **ground cumin**

1 teaspoon **ground coriander**

1 tablespoon freshly chopped **mint**

4 **pitta breads** or **flatbreads**, see p214

2 tablespoons **sweet chilli sauce**

2 tablespoons **Greek yoghurt**

1 **Little Gem lettuce**, chopped

5cm piece **cucumber**, sliced

1 Put the kebab ingredients in a food processor and blitz until everything is chopped. Season well with salt and pepper.

2 With oil on your hands, form into 4 sausage shapes.

3 Make your flatbreads, see p214.

4 Air fry the kebabs at 200°C for 10 minutes or until nicely browned.
🌡 *Internal temperature 70°C*

5 Meanwhile, mix the sweet chilli sauce and yoghurt.

6 Serve the kebabs with the lettuce, cucumber and flatbreads.

Single basket?

Either, just use pitta breads, or make your flat breads ahead of time.

Time	Serves	£/person
30 mins	2	£1.49

Flatbreads in your air fryer

Scan for video

Loaded Lamb Roast

1 **onion**, quartered

400g **new potatoes**, halved

3 **medium carrots**, cut into sticks

200g **parsnips**, cut into sticks

1 tablespoon freshly chopped **rosemary**

2 cloves **garlic**, finely grated

1 teaspoon **olive oil**

600g **boneless leg of lamb**

1 tablespoon **mint sauce**

Single basket?

Air fry the vegetables first, then remove and cover with foil to keep warm while the lamb cooks. At the end, if needed, reheat the vegetables in the air fryer.

1 In a large bowl, toss together the onion, potatoes, carrots and parsnips with a little oil. Air fry at 180°C for 25 minutes or until nicely browned.

2 Meanwhile, in a small bowl, combine the rosemary, garlic and oil, then rub all over the lamb.

3 In the second basket, air fry the lamb, fat side down, at 180°C for 10 minutes. Turn over and air fry for another 10 minutes or until nicely browned.

🌡 *Internal temperature 68-72°C*

4 Remove the lamb from the air fryer and leave to rest, then slice.

5 In a large bowl, toss everything together along with the mint sauce.

	Time	Serves	£/person
184	30 mins	2	£4.31

Lamb Cobbler

1 **small onion**, sliced
2 **medium carrots**, chopped
1 clove **garlic**, chopped
250g **minced lamb**
1 tablespoon **plain flour**
125g **mushrooms**, sliced
1 mug (300ml) **boiling water**
1 **lamb stock cube**
1 teaspoon **dried rosemary**

Cobbler
½ mug (100g) **self-raising flour**
¼ mug (40g) **suet**
1 teaspoon **dried basil**
¼ mug (75ml) **water**

1 **egg**, beaten
1 mug (150g) defrosted **frozen peas**

1 In a loaf tin in your basket, add the onion, carrots and garlic and air fry at 200°C for 5 minutes, or until the onion begins to brown.

2 Add the lamb and air fry for 10 minutes, or until the beef begins to brown.

3 Mix in the flour and air fry for 2 minutes.

4 Add the mushrooms, boiling water, stock cube and rosemary. Season well with salt and pepper.

5 Tightly cover the loaf tin with foil and air fry for 20 minutes.

6 Mix the dry cobbler ingredients in a bowl. Add enough water to bring the mixture together into a ball, then form into 4 balls.

7 After the 20 minutes, remove the foil and place the cobblers on top of the meat mixture. Brush with the beaten egg and return to the air fryer, uncovered, for 15 minutes, or until the cobblers are browned.

8 Meanwhile, cook your peas, see p213.

Time	Serves	£/person
60 mins	2	£2.93

Lamb Meatball Casserole

3 **medium potatoes**, cut into small chunks

1 **onion**, sliced

2 cloves **garlic**, chopped

250g **minced lamb**

1 teaspoon **ground cumin**

1 teaspoon **ground coriander**

1 teaspoon **smoked paprika**

350g **passata**

1 mug (150g) defrosted **frozen peas**

100g **fresh spinach**, roughly chopped

Single basket?

Air fry the potatoes first, and keep them warm in foil while you make the meatballs. Once you've completed step 5, add the cooked potatoes on top and air fry for a further 5 minutes to warm through.

1 Toss the potatoes in a little oil, season with salt and pepper, and air fry at 180°C for 20 minutes or until browned.

2 Meanwhile, in the other basket, with the crisper tray removed, air fry the onion and garlic at 200°C for 5 minutes, or until the onion begins to brown.

3 In a bowl, combine the mince, cumin, coriander and paprika. Form into 10 meatballs.

4 Add the meatballs to the onion and garlic and air fry for 10 minutes, or until they begin to brown. Turn them once or twice to ensure they cook evenly.

🌡 *Internal temperature 70°C*

5 Add the passata and return to the air fryer for 5 minutes to heat through.

6 Cook the peas, see p213.

7 Add the cooked peas and spinach, and stir until the spinach wilts. Season with salt and pepper.

Time	Serves	£/person
30 mins	2	£2.40

Baked Cheesecake

50g **butter**
150g **Hobnobs**
300g **cream cheese**
50g **caster sugar**
½ teaspoon **vanilla extract**
2 **eggs**

1 In a circular shallow baking tin, add the butter and air fry at 140°C for 2 minutes to melt.

2 In a food processor (or in a sandwich bag, using a rolling pin), break up the biscuits into crumbs. Stir into the melted butter and press down evenly into the tin.

3 In a large bowl, mix the cream cheese, sugar and vanilla extract.

4 Add one egg at a time, mixing well after each addition.

5 Pour the mixture over the biscuit base and air fry at 140°C for 30 minutes.

6 Leave to cool completely, before carefully removing from the tin. If you don't have a loose-bottomed tin (like we don't), slide a small knife around the edges to loosen. Place a plate on top, flip the tin over, then place another plate on top to turn it back the right way up.

Time	Serves	£/person
45 mins	4	£0.91

Chilli Chocolate Melting Pots

50g **butter**, diced

60g **dark chocolate**, broken up

¼ teaspoon **chilli powder**

1 **egg**

¼ mug (60g) **caster sugar**

1 tablespoon **plain flour**

pinch of **salt**

2 tablespoons **crème fraîche**

1 Add the butter, chocolate and chilli powder to a shallow baking tin and air fry at 180°C for 2 minutes, or until the chocolate has melted. Stir occasionally to check. Set aside to cool.

2 In a large bowl, whisk the egg and sugar together until smooth and pale.

3 Gently fold in the melted chocolate mixture, followed by the flour and salt.

4 Grease your ramekins well with butter. Pour in the mixture and air fry at 180°C for 10 minutes.

5 Either eat directly from the ramekins, or carefully remove them by sliding a small knife around the edges, placing a plate over the top, and flipping them over.

6 Serve with crème fraîche.

Time	Serves	£/person
20 mins	2	£0.70

Summer Fruit Crumble

Filling

250g **frozen summer fruits**

1 teaspoon **vanilla extract**

1 tablespoon **caster sugar**

Topping

4 **ginger biscuits**, broken up a little

1/2 teaspoon **ground ginger**

1/2 mug (50g) **oats**

25g **butter**

1 tablespoon **ground almonds**

1 tablespoon **caster sugar**

ice cream

1 Add the filling ingredients to a shallow baking tin in your basket. Air fry at 180°C for 8 minutes.

2 Blitz the topping ingredients until you have a something resembling breadcrumbs.

3 Pour the topping over the fruit and air fry at 180°C for 10 minutes or until lightly browned.

4 Serve with ice cream.

Time	Serves	£/person
25 mins	2	£1.17

Pain Au Chocolat Pudding

1 **egg**
4 tablespoons **Greek yoghurt**
1 tablespoon **honey**
1 teaspoon **vanilla extract**
4 **pains au chocolat**, halved

1 Mix together, the egg, yoghurt, honey and vanilla extract.

2 Arrange the pain au chocolat in a shallow baking tin.

3 Pour the egg mixture over the top of the pain au chocolat.

4 Cover with foil and air fry at 200°C for 10 minutes. Remove the foil and air fry for a further 3 minutes, or until things begin to brown and the egg mixture is set.

Time	Serves	£/person
15 mins	4	£0.30

All Butter Shortbread

70g **butter**, softened

30g **caster sugar**

½ mug (90g) **plain flour**

1 teaspoon **granulated sugar**

1 In a large bowl, mix together the softened butter and caster sugar until smooth.

2 Mix in the flour until fully combined.

3 Bring the mixture together with your hands and press it down into a shallow baking tin.

4 Using a fork, gently make indentations in the shortbread.

5 Air fry at 160°C for 15 minutes or until very lightly browned.

6 Sprinkle with granulated sugar as soon as you take it out of the air fryer. Score lines in the soft shortbread.

7 Leave to cool completely before removing from the tray.

Time	Serves	£/person
20 mins	4	£0.17

Baked Peach & Pistachios

25g **butter**

2 **ripe peaches**, halved and stone removed

1 tablespoon **honey**

1/4 teaspoon **ground cinnamon**

25g **pistachios**

vanilla ice cream or **crème fraîche**

1 Divide the butter between the peach halves, placing it in the centre of each, cut side up.

2 Drizzle with honey and sprinkle with cinnamon. Place the peaches in a shallow baking tin and air fry at 200°C for 5 minutes.

3 Sprinkle over the pistachios and return to the air fryer for 3 minutes, or until the pistachios are lightly browned.

4 Serve with ice cream or a dollop of crème fraîche.

Time	Serves	£/person
15 mins	2	£1.51

Peanut Butter Brownie

50g **butter**, cut into cubes

1/3 mug (60g) **brown sugar**

50g **dark chocolate**, broken up

1/4 mug (40g) **self-raising flour**

1 **egg**, beaten

2 teaspoons **smooth peanut butter**

1 Put the butter, sugar, and chocolate in a small heatproof container and air fry at 160°C, checking every minute and stirring, until everything has melted.

2 In a mixing bowl, combine the melted chocolate mixture with the flour.

3 Add the beaten egg and mix until smooth.

4 Pour into a shallow, lined baking tin.

5 Add small blobs of peanut butter to the top and swirl with a knife to make a pattern.

6 Air fry at 160°C for 15 minutes.

7 Leave to cool for as long as you can, before carefully removing from the tray.

Time	Serves	£/person
20 mins	4	£0.34

Chocolate Chip Cookies

30g **butter**, softened

30g **caster sugar**

½ teaspoon **vanilla extract**

¼ mug (50g) **self-raising flour**

¼ teaspoon **baking powder**

20g **chocolate chips**

1 In a large bowl, mix together the butter and sugar until smooth.

2 Mix in the rest of the ingredients.

3 Form the mixture into 2 balls and press each one down gently onto a small square of baking paper.

4 Air fry at 180°C for 10 minutes or until golden. Leave to cool completely before lifting them out of the basket.

Time	Serves	£/person
15 mins	2	£0.34

Stapl
Refer

es &
ence

RICE...

In the Air fryer?

1 Add your rice to a loaf tin, along with double the volume of boiling water. Season with salt, or as the recipe suggests. Give it one stir, then tightly cover with foil.

2 Air fry at 200°C for 20 minutes, then check. Tip the tin slightly to see if there's any liquid left. If not, you're done. If there's still some liquid remaining, simply cover with foil again and return to the air fryer for a few more minutes.

Coconut Rice:
If you're making coconut rice (where the liquid is coconut milk), you'll need to add around 5 more minutes to the cooking time.

In the Saucepan?

1 Add your rice to a saucepan with **double the volume of boiling water**. Season with salt, or as the recipe suggests. Give it one stir, then cover with a lid.

2 Bring to the boil, then reduce to a gentle simmer for 10 minutes, or until all the liquid has evaporated.

Rice in your air fryer

Scan for video

VEG...

In The Air Fryer?

'Steaming' broccoli

There are so many vegetables you can cook directly in your air fryer, and you'll get a lovely browned, crispy result – which is great. But there are times when you just want tender veg without all the browning. Air fryers can actually be used as mini steamers, which is brilliant.

1 Find a loaf tin that fits in your air fryer (see p24). Alternatively, if you have some heavy-duty foil, you can make a foil parcel, which works just as well – just be careful it doesn't spring a leak!

2 Trim your broccoli and add it to the loaf tin, along with 60ml of boiling water.

3 Tightly cover the top of the tin with foil, crimping around the edges to make a seal.

4 Air fry for 9 minutes, then test if it's cooked how you like it. If not, return it to the air fryer with the foil back on for a few more minutes.

Some rough steaming times

You can use the same method above for a variation of veg, just change the time: Asparagus (8 minutes), mangetout (7 minutes), cabbage (9 minutes), kale (8 minutes) and green beans (8 minutes).

<u>NOT</u> In The Air Fryer?

Broccoli

1 In a medium saucepan with a lid, add the broccoli to about a mug (300ml) of salted, boiling water – no need to cover it completely.

2 With the lid on, simmer for 5 minutes, or until the broccoli is tender. This method effectively steams the broccoli rather than boiling it, which helps retain more flavour.

Peas

There's a bit of a myth out there that causes people to overcook peas. Frozen peas are actually cooked before they're frozen, so they only need warming through - not cooking again. In this book, we recommend the following method:

In a large bowl, cover your defrosted peas with boiling water. Leave them to sit for 3 minutes, then drain. Simple.

Mangetout

Mangetout are a bit different to frozen peas – they do need a little cooking, but not much. The good news is you can cheat by slicing them lengthways to help them cook more quickly.

1 Add your sliced mangetout to a large bowl and cover with plenty of boiling water.

2 Leave to stand for 5 minutes, then drain. They'll still have a nice crunch, but will be lightly cooked and ready to go.

Veg in your air fryer
Scan for video

Flatbreads

⅓ mug (100ml) **Greek yoghurt**

1 teaspoon **chilli flakes** (½ if you don't like it spicy)

1 teaspoon **cumin seeds**

200g **self-raising flour**

Flatbreads in your air fryer
Scan for video

1 Put all the ingredients in a food processor, season well with salt and pepper, and blitz until smooth. Add extra water if needed (only 1 tablespoon at a time) to create a soft dough. It should take around 3 tablespoons.

2 Divide the mixture into 4 and, with oil on your hands, press into flat breads. No need for a rolling pin.

3 Air fry at 200°C for 6–8 minutes or until lightly browned.

Mash

On The Hob

1 Peel (optional) and chop your potatoes into even-sized chunks.

2 Place the potatoes in a large saucepan and cover with cold, salted water. Bring to the boil.

3 Once boiling, simmer for around 10 minutes, or until the potatoes are tender - check with a fork. Cooking time will vary depending on the size of the chunks.

4 Once cooked, drain using a colander, return to the pan, and add butter (and cheese if the recipe asks for it) and season with salt and pepper.

5 Mash until smooth.

In An Air Fryer

1 Make a shallow cross-shaped slit in each potato.

2 Air fry at 180°C for 45 minutes or until soft and cooked all the way through.

3 Remove from the air fryer and scoop out the flesh with a spoon into a bowl. Add butter (and cheese if the recipe asks for it) and season with salt and pepper.

4 Mash until nice and smooth.

Mash in your air fryer
Scan for video

Reference Chart

Food	Air Fryer Temperature	Cook Time	Internal Temperature
Beef burger (homemade)	200°C	10 minutes	70°C
Chicken – Breast	200°C	12 minutes	74°C
Chicken – homemade burger	190°C	12 minutes	74°C
Chicken – homemade nuggets	200°C	10 minutes	74°C
Chicken – Large Leg	190°C	35 minutes	74°C
Chicken – Thighs	200°C	18 minutes	74°C
Chicken – Whole	180°C	60 minutes	74°C
Chicken – Wings	180°C	25 minutes	74°C
Fish – Cod	200°C	8 minutes	63°C
Fish – Mackerel	200°C	5 minutes	63°C
Fish – Prawns	200°C	5 minutes	63°C
Fish – Salmon	200°C	8 minutes	50-63°C
Lamb – Boneless leg (600g)	180°C	20 minutes	60-80°C
Lamb burger (homemade)	200°C	10 minutes	70°C
Lamb chops	200°C	10 minutes	60-70°C

Food	Air Fryer Temperature	Cook Time	Internal Temperature
Pork – Bacon	200°C	7 minutes	70°C
Pork Belly	200°C	15 minutes	77°C
Pork chipolatas	200°C	10 minutes	71°C
Pork chops	200°C	12 minutes	75°C
Pork sausages	200°C	15 minutes	71°C
Potato – Baked	180°C	45 minutes	98°C
Potatoes – Baby new (halved)	180°C	20 minutes	98°C
Potatoes – Chips	180°C	25 minutes	98°C
Potatoes – Mini Roast	180°C	20 minutes	98°C
Potatoes – Traditional Roast	180°C	30 minutes	98°C
Potatoes – Wedges	180°C	30 minutes	98°C

Steaks	Internal Temperature
Rare	50°C
Medium Rare	55°C
Medium	60°C
Medium Well	65°C
Well Done	70°C

index

Subscribe

Get recipes, tips and be the first to hear about new books.

© Joy May & Tim May 2025

Published by: inTrade (GB) Ltd

Contact: us@noshbooks.com

ISBN: 978-1-8383010-2-6

Printed in China

1st Edition: September 2025

Authors: Joy May & Tim May

Recipe Development and Styling: Tim May

Photography & Design: Milk Bottle Designs

Editor: Ron May

Proof-reader: Fran Maciver

Recipe Costs

The recipe costs in this book are an average between Tesco and Sainsbury's at the time of writing. To keep the pricing relevant, we aim to update them each time we do a new print run. Latest costs are as at April 2025.